Six Types of Teachers

Recruiting, Retaining, and Mentoring the Best

Douglas J. Fiore and Todd Whitaker

EYE ON EDUCATION
6 DEPOT WAY WEST, SUITE 106
LARCHMONT, NY 10538
(914) 833–0551
(914) 833–0761 fax
www.eyeoneducation.com

Library of Congress Cataloging-in-Publication Data

Fiore, Douglas J., 1966-
Six types of teachers : recruiting, retaining, and mentoring the best / Douglas J. Fiore & Todd Whitaker.
    p. cm.
Includes bibliographical references.
ISBN 1-930556-85-3
1. School personnel management. 2. Teachers—Recruiting. 3. Teacher turnover—Prevention. I. Whitaker, Todd, 1959- II. Title.
LB2832.F56 2005
371.2'01—dc22

2004015724

10 9 8 7 6 5 4 3 2 1

Editorial and production services provided by
Richard H. Adin Freelance Editorial Services
52 Oakwood Blvd., Poughkeepsie, NY 12603-4112
(914-471-3566)

Meet the Authors

Dr. Douglas J. Fiore has spent the last 17 years in public education working as a teacher, a principal, and a university professor. He is the author of *School Community Relations, Introduction to Educational Administration: Standards, Theories, and Practice,* and *Creating Connections for Better Schools: How Leaders Enhance School Culture.* He is co-author with Dr. Todd Whitaker of *Dealing with Difficult Parents (And with Parents in Difficult Situations).*

Doug also has written numerous articles and has been interviewed by several newspaper and magazine reporters covering educational issues throughout the United States. In addition, Doug provides staff development to many school districts, and is a presenter at many state and national conferences for both teachers and administrators.

Doug and his wife Lisa live in Midlothian, Virginia, with their three daughters, Meagan, Amy, and Katherine.

Dr. Todd Whitaker is a Professor of Educational Leadership at Indiana State University in Terre Haute, Indiana. A former teacher and principal, he is internationally recognized as an inspirational and distinguished speaker.

Dr. Whitaker's work has been published in the areas of teacher leadership, instructional improvement, change, leadership effectiveness, technology, and middle level practices. His books include the number one best seller, *What Great Teachers Do Differently,* and other best selling titles including *Great Quotes for Great Educators, What Great Principals Do Differently, Dealing with Difficult Teachers Motivating & Inspiring Teachers, Dealing with Difficult Parents, Feeling Great!,* and *Teaching Matters.*

Todd and his wife Beth are the parents of Katherine, Madeline, and Harrison.

Table of Contents

Section I The Keyword Is *Quality* 1

1 Who Moved My Teacher? 3
Why We Need Quality Teachers 6
Two Ways to Improve Our Schools—Two Ways
    to Weaken Them 8
What Lies Ahead? 10

2 Irreplaceable Parts 11
Six Types of Teachers 13
Valuing the Irreplaceables 14
Solidifying the Solids 16
Managing the Replacement Level 18
We Are Not in a Vacuum 20
Weighing the Peripherals 21

3 Opportunity Costs 23
Opportunity Costs 25
What Did We Lose? 26
What Else Can We Get? 27
What If the Current Staff Were Applicants? 27
The Strength of Stability 29
The Value of Experience 30

Section II Why Teachers Leave 31

4 From the Mouths of Teachers 33
The Facts about Teacher Retention 35
Why Is This Happening? 37
A Culture of Support 38
It's All in the Atmosphere 40

5 Are We Talking about the Great Ones? 43
Recognizing the Achievement of the Great Ones 47
Assisting Great Teachers in Personal and
    Professional Growth 48

Section III **51**

Creating, Fostering, and Sustaining Quality **51**

6   Building a Quality Culture **53**
   A Culture That Feels Good 55
   What Should I Do? 56
   Improving Classroom Culture
         by Improving School Culture 60
   Go Fish 61

7   Making Teaching Rewarding **63**
   If You Don't Have Something Nice to Say... 66
   Perception Is Reality 67
   Didn't I Just See You? 68
   But I Don't Have Time 69
   Making it OK to Care 70
   Something Positive in My Mailbox? 71

8   Keeping the Great Ones Motivated **73**
   Can I Motivate from the Outside? 77
   A Final Thought about Motivation 81

Section IV **83**

Adding Quality **83**

9   Adding Quality—Expanding Our Pool **85**
   Searching for Irreplaceables 87
   The Emotional Pull 88
   The Known Quantity 89
   Hiring People Better Than Ourselves 90
   The Good Fit 90
   Arbitrary Factors—Narrowing the Pool 91
   Understanding Our Needs 92

10 Finding and Choosing the Best **93**
   The Screening 96
   The Reference Check 96
   Finding the Leaders 97
   The Neutral View 97
   Interview Questions 98
   Would You Know Whom to Hire? 98

What Would You Do If? 99
Setting Expectations 100
Do You Want to Be the Best? 101

11 Inducting New Teachers 103
New Staff Induction and Orientation 106
Mentor Programs 108
Ongoing Orientation 109
Cultivating Leadership 110

Section V The Impact of Other Stakeholders . . . 113

12 Supporting Teachers in Parent Interactions . . . 115
Cheers or Boos 117
Soothing the Savage Beast 118
Staff Development Focused on Parents 120
Do They Feel Supported? 122

13 Nurturing Student—Teacher Relationships . . 125
Recognizing Success in Student–Teacher
    Relationships 128
Student–Teacher Relationships and the Six Types
    of Teachers 130
Nurturing Solid Relationships 131

14 Building a Family Atmosphere through Purposeful Mentoring 133
Induction That Sticks 135
Why Focus on Mentoring? 138
Mentoring the Mentors 139
When Does Mentoring End? 142

15 Teaching: The Most Important Profession . . . 145
Retaining Quality Teachers 152

If you would like information about inviting Doug Fiore
to speak to your group, please contact him at
doug@dougfiore.com
or www.dougfiore.com
or (804) 647-1945 or (804) 897-9884

If you would like information about inviting Todd Whitaker
to speak to your group, please contact him at
t-whitaker@indstate.edu
or www.toddwhitaker.com
or (812) 237-2904

Section I

The Keyword Is *Quality*

1

Who Moved My Teacher?

Most educational leaders have read the classic book by Spencer Johnson (1998), *Who Moved My Cheese?* This book is a wonderful resource for developing an understanding of why change is so frightening to people. At times, even if we know that what we are doing is not working, we are so resistant and fearful of doing something different that we continue to plow ahead in the same unproductive manner. Eventually we may completely run out of resources (in the book, cheese), so we are finally forced into trying something else—or ceasing to exist. A parallel challenge faces our schools.

For years, whenever a teacher left a district, the personnel director would just go to the file cabinet stuffed with applications, pull out the ones relevant to the position, and choose from the wealth of options. Although sometimes we did not end up with the best, we were still able to find someone to fill the slot. And if we really got desperate, we could always hire someone from the substitute teacher list. That person might not have been particularly good, but at least we always had that option. This list provided dozens of readily available teachers.

But two things have happened simultaneously that have forced us to look for new paths. First, expectations have changed. No longer can we accept "average" from any of our teachers. Although our schools continue to improve, the expectations for schools escalate even more rapidly. Handing out worksheets and watching videos may have been acceptable long ago, but not today. Teachers must be able to work effectively with a diverse group of students. We can no longer accept a poor teacher—nor should we. Every child is expected to be able to achieve at increasingly higher rates. This may be a stressful expectation, but it is one that we all are required to reach. This alone is a change that may have caused some self-examination of practices.

Second, the pool of potential applicants has been drying up rapidly. Although the number of special education students is rising, the roster of teacher candidates with this certification is dwindling and in some cases disappearing. There are higher math requirements and fewer math teachers. Colleges expect four years of foreign language in high school, yet schools struggle to find even one teacher certified for Introductory French.

The expectations, demands, and responsibilities placed on teachers are ever growing, while the number of people coming into the profession is shrinking. Turnover woes mount, while alternatives disappear. We still can head to the same file cabinet of applicants, but the drawers aren't as full. As a last resort we pick up the sub list, but we quickly realize we cannot even find enough warm bodies to serve as substitute teachers! Expectations climb and resources drop. The old comfortable path no longer works. We would like to reflect on the good old days, but we just don't have time—and the good old days are not coming back. The demands on everyone have increased, and it seems as though some of our best people are bailing out. Even when we find sharp young teachers, they leave after only a year or two.

What has happened? Why did it happen? More important, is there anything we can do to counteract it? This book helps us understand what we need to do, why we need to do it, and how we can improve our own leadership skills to retain our best and brightest teachers.

Why We Need Quality Teachers

One of the challenges facing educational leaders is that everyone is an expert about schools. All our parents and community members attended school at one time or another. Therefore, they officially anoint themselves as experts. Their own experiences have helped shape their personal beliefs about what constitutes a good teacher. Even though everyone enters schools with differing expectations and experiences, we all leave having been influenced, one way or another, by our teachers.

Years after leaving school, each of us can recall many of the educators we called our teachers—our best teachers and those that did not rank as high on our list of favorites. Although people attend a wide variety of schools in thousands of locales, often our experiences are more similar than different. We can all recall the classroom where the most learning took place—not just book learning, but learning about life. And even when we might not remember definitions or equations, we can easily rekindle the feelings we had in that classroom.

In some classrooms, we felt warm and welcomed. In others, we felt intimidated and uncomfortable. Some teachers made us want to try; others stifled our enthusiasm. Even the way the students treated each other varied from class to class. Our best teachers developed environments where pupils respected their peers. Others let sarcasm and putdowns rule the day. Although our classmates are an important part of our memories, it is the teachers who determined what we learned about working together.

For years, people have discussed the idea of replacing teachers, arguing that the need for a "real person" in each classroom is archaic. Everything from individual student readings to videotapes and computers have been cited as eliminating the need for the teacher. Well-meaning though these efforts may have been, they have only reinforced the value of the teacher. Other things can supplement and support a teacher, but nothing can replace the personal touch that a good teacher provides. Not only is there an obvious relationship between student learning and instruction, but there is also an additional intrinsic connection between teachers and students. In a study of teacher self-concept and student self-concept, Lumpa (1997) found a significant relationship between the two. The more positively teachers feel about themselves, the more positively the students view themselves.

Even schools and districts that have no intention of doing without teachers face the challenge of losing talented staff members, for reasons we will explore further in Section II. Coupled with a decline in the number of people entering the teaching profession, this has created a crisis, especially in some locales. But even the most fortunate areas that have an abundance of applicants still encounter frequent shortages in special education, mathematics, and sciences. And even more important than the *quantity* of teachers and potential educators is their *quality*. As a principal, if I have an opening in my school, I would like to have 25 or 30 applicants to choose from—but I would rather have one outstanding candidate than a dozen average ones.

Retaining teachers is important. However, retaining our best teachers is essential. The thinner the applicant pool, the more critical it is to preserve our current staff members. And the better our current staff members, the more we need to work to keep them in our schools.

Two Ways to Improve Our Schools— Two Ways to Weaken Them

School improvement can come in many formats from a variety of sources. We can apply for grants to generate additional funding. All schools continually look for new programs that will enable them to increase student achievement and enhance learning. There are a multitude of different ideas to improve student behavior. All of these are viable options to make a school better. But if we are really looking for dramatic improvement, we have two basic options: We can *hire better teachers* or we can *improve the teachers* already in the school. Although other factors can support or refine the skills of our existing staff, the people in a school are going to determine the quality of that school. If a poor teacher leaves, and we hire an energetic, talented replacement, the impact is immediate and remarkable. A new dynamo affects not only the students in the classroom but also potentially the entire school.

If we understand this fundamental concept—that the quality of the people will ultimately determine the quality of the organization—then we must also recognize the converse. The fastest way for a school to decline is to lose its best teachers. Deteriorating morale and a loss of effectiveness among the current teachers may cause a slow slide, but losing an excellent teacher makes a difference right away. A school, district, or state faced with a scarcity of highly qualified applicants (or even applicants in general!) must worry about the likelihood of replacing each departing staff member with someone less effective. And just as replacing a poor teacher with an outstanding educator has an impact far beyond the classroom, replacing one of our best staff members from a weak pool of candidates can have a reverberating effect.

Understanding the value of our existing staff is important. If our school is like most schools, our teachers exhibit a wide array of abilities. Some teachers are irreplaceable; others may bring a negative energy to the school. And in most places, the vast majority are somewhere in between. Being aware of the effectiveness of everyone in our school is an important first step in making sure we work to retain our most valuable resources—our quality teachers. In addition, every administrator needs to be aware of the quality of potential replacements. If the candidate pool is teeming with excellent candidates who would also choose our district, then our potential to hire outstanding teachers may be quite different from that in another setting.

The comparison between the teachers we have and potential replacements can help define which teachers we need to work most effectively to retain. The subject area—special education, elementary, foreign language—makes a difference, as does the desirability of our school and district. Some rural areas may face a shortage of candidates, whereas a heavily populated area might find teacher retention a greater challenge. In a small district, we may struggle with three openings, little local appeal, and few candidates. In a major metropolitan area, our challenge may be how to fill the annual thousand vacancies and counter the perception of troubled schools. Both settings can benefit by retaining their best and brightest. Even with a rich pool of applicants to choose from, if we lose our very best staff members, we will often find it difficult or impossible to replace them in quality.

What Lies Ahead?

This book is divided into five major sections. Section I helps to build an understanding of the importance of quality teachers, describes the various talent levels of teachers, and presents a framework to determine how essential it may be to retain a particular teacher. Section II addresses why teachers leave, based on information from several studies. Section III helps educational leaders understand how to build the quality of the faculty in our schools, and Section IV provides ideas on adding quality and cultivating ways to make sure we keep our positive new additions. Finally, Section V examines the impact that others can have on teacher satisfaction and determines positive ways that school leaders can influence teachers' views of the profession. Providing support for teachers in their interactions with parents and students can be a key factor in teachers choosing to remain in the profession. In addition, Section V provides reinforcement for all educators to feel valued on a continual basis.

Retaining our current staff can help offset the dearth of applicants that schools now face. By keeping our current staff, we can have continuity and avoid desperate searches for replacements. To meet the increasing demands all of us face, *we must keep our best teachers.* Retaining our best and brightest teachers puts us on track to make our schools better. Furthermore, it holds the key to meeting the new accountability demands all schools now face. We hope this book will give you an understanding of how to identify and cultivate quality teachers, as well as some tools for building a quality school culture and keeping your best and brightest teachers motivated in their work.

2

Irreplaceable Parts

As administrators, at times we have difficulty viewing our faculty objectively. We have worked and struggled side by side with our teachers; even though some of them may have pretty obvious warts, we still care about them as people. Caring is a wonderful trait that every educational leader should have. However, if we view our faculty through rose-colored glasses, we may lose sight of the needs of the most important people—the students. Although district evaluation tools make some attempt to objectify people, they are a guide at best and unhelpful at worst.

Businesses often have more concrete determinants of success. A salesperson may generate a certain dollar amount in revenue each year. Performance quotas—the number of test-drives or cold calls a month—offer a fairly objective basis for comparison. Finding objective criteria is much more challenging when the job involves working with students and other adults. Test scores represent a common attempt at measuring performance, but we all know how many variables come into play using this standard. We need a better method.

In this chapter, we present descriptions that offer a framework for neutral assessment and comparison of teacher effectiveness. One reason we need this neutral measure for understanding the quality of teachers is so we can determine where to focus our retention efforts; another is so we can evaluate the potential of candidates to replace any teachers that we lose. Whenever we think about retaining teachers, we must also ask, "What else do I have to choose from?"

Six Types of Teachers

The framework presented here encourages school leaders to evaluate the teachers in their schools and districts in terms of which ones they really want to keep and which they may be better able to replace. Looking at teachers in this light enhances the school leader's ability to view them objectively. The framework describes teachers in three general groups, with six specific labels:

- ◆ The Irreplaceables
  - WOW (walks on water)—the role model
  - Impacter—great in the classroom
- ◆ The Solids
  - Stabilizer—solid at everything
  - Dow Joneser—pluses and minuses
- ◆ Replacement Level
  - Harmless—no complaints, little benefit
  - Negative Force—addition by subtraction

Valuing the Irreplaceables

We refer to the most talented teachers in our schools as the Irreplaceables. If one of these people leaves, we have little chance of hiring someone else as talented and effective. Al Burr (1993) describes the people in this category as superstars—the teachers that parents seek out for their children and that many students would rate as their best teachers.

The irreplaceable teachers often represent a very small percentage of a faculty or staff—5% to 10%. Depending on the school's size, this may mean just two teachers or a dozen, but all of them are at the very top of the talent pile.

We subdivide the people in this rare group into WOWs (the ones who *walk on water*) and Impacters. The difference between the two lies in the effect they have on the school as a whole.

A key characteristic of the WOW teachers is their ability to lead others in a positive manner. They earn the respect of their peers, who may work to emulate them. But even more important, they have the knack of teaching teachers—helping other teachers become more effective. Above and beyond their richly positive influence on the students in their classrooms, they help make the entire school better.

These individuals, while incredibly valuable, are also at high risk to leave. The same talents that make them able to interact positively with students, peers, and supervisors would serve them equally well in another school or in any work setting. Losing a WOW or adding one to your faculty can have a tremendous effect that ripples throughout the school.

The second group—Impacters—may be just as talented as the WOWs, but their impact is limited to the students. They may be considered the best classroom teachers in the school or district. In addition, their willingness to do extracurricular activities with children makes their effectiveness go beyond the classroom. However, the group they affect is the students, not other staff members.

This is not at all a criticism of an Impacter. Having this level of ability to work with students is marvelous and a rare commodity. However, it also provides a framework for understanding the strengths of an Impacter as well as differences between groups of teachers.

Losing a WOW is a schoolwide loss. Although the loss in the classroom is significant, the reduction in leadership among peer teachers may be even more devastating. Within a grade level, team, or department, often one or two personalities determine the attitude and morale of everyone involved. A negative leader can suppress the efforts and motivation of others. A positive teacher leader—WOW—can equally shift the group in a productive direction. If this person is truly special, the loss can be comparable to losing several teachers, because others may not have as much energy and direction after their peer leader departs.

The Impacter is also difficult to replace but not necessarily for the same reasons. Many times it is the parents who miss an Impacter most. They saw what this teacher did with one child and hope for the same with a younger sibling. Students and parents will probably compare the new staff member with the outstanding educator who left. Everyone in the school may have recognized this teacher's quality, but the departure does not affect the other teachers as directly. Indeed, other staff members may even have felt a degree of jealousy because of how students and families regarded this talented colleague.

However, as principal, you have no doubt that the Impacter's departure will make a difference to the students who would have had that teacher.

Although Irreplaceables are just that, irreplaceable, we as school leaders need to understand the effect of losing (or hiring) a WOW or an Impacter. This enables us to sharpen our focus on the teachers we can least afford to lose.

Solidifying the Solids

After the upper echelon comes the largest group of teachers and staff in our schools, the Solids. Typically they represent about 80% to 90% of our faculty and staff. They do most of the teaching in our schools—and most of the secretarial work, cooking, bus driving, and maintenance. By and large, the Solids count as dependable, hardworking contributors to the good of the school. As you might expect, their personalities vary widely. Some Solids are friendly and cheerful in the teachers' lounge and pretty good in the classroom. Others are well above average in their work with students but don't take on many extra responsibilities. Many Solids do a pretty good job pretty much of the time—but they lack that certain spark that would make them Irreplaceable. Maybe they have less charisma; maybe they don't go the extra mile. Perhaps they just need a few more years of experience to become Irreplaceable. But for now, they are in the large constituency nicely known as the Solids.

When an Irreplaceable leaves, you will probably have trouble hiring someone as talented. Nudging that standard down a little, a quick description of a Solid might be that if two or three of them left your organization, you would probably break even in terms of ability when you replaced them. That is, if three Solids left a school, you could most likely employ three others of about the same effectiveness. Sometimes you can do a little better, and other times a little worse, but in general, that is what the level of talent in the world is like—the Solids.

Please understand that we do not intend this description to be at all mean-spirited or insulting. We might really miss

Mr. Jones's jokes or Mrs. Henry's helpful spirit. Conversely, we might not miss Mr. Baker's body language at staff meetings. But in terms of talent, they fall into the large group of staff members that we have labeled as Solids.

We can also identify two subgroups of Solids: the Stabilizers and the Dow Jonesers. One is not necessarily better than the other, but they are quite different. With Stabilizers, what you see is what you get. Basically, they are the same every day. Whatever their talents, they perform consistently. They can be pretty good in the classroom, pretty good as coaches, and pretty good in enhancing the climate of the school. Monday to Friday, September to May, you know what to expect of them, and you get it. The talent of the half-dozen Stabilizers in your school may vary a great deal, but you can count on their consistency. Some of your Stabilizers may be almost Irreplaceable. Others may border on the Harmless. But once you have evaluated them, you know what you have.

Dow Jonesers don't fall into such neat categories. The legendary basketball announcer Dick Vitale coined this term to describe inconsistent players—the ones who may score 20 points one game and 6 the next. Teachers, too, may vary from day to day; we also describe as Dow Jonesers the staff members whose talents vary depending on the task at hand. Some may be good in the classroom but disorganized when it comes to extracurricular activities. Others may be fantastic as track coaches but rather humdrum in the classroom.

In addition, a Dow Joneser might teach pretty well for the first three-quarters of the school year but run out of steam as spring turns to summer. He could have unpredictable ups and downs; she could reliably manage the janitorial staff but lose her temper on occasion. Weighing the ups versus the downs will help determine how much you want to retain a Dow Joneser. Maybe the ups are so valuable that your goal is to smooth the rough edges. Perhaps you want to limit the situations where Dow Jonesers are not as effective and increase those where they shine. Potentially, the downs are so negative that the ups are not worth the trouble. You have to decide that for yourself. But understanding and even being able to articulate the description of a staff member in this manner may help clarify whether you want to retain or employ someone of any category, including the Dow Joneser.

Managing the Replacement Level

The third group of staff members is a little easier to identify, but they may be harder to work with. Bill James, author of the *Baseball Abstract* (1996), describes replacement level players as those that are barely in the major leagues. In other words, if one of them retired, many players even in the minor leagues are as good if not better. Batting .240 may be "not bad," but we can always find someone at least as good and possibly a great deal better.

This is sort of what a Replacement Level teacher is like. Typically, 5% to 10% of our faculty and staff are Replacement Level—the other end of the bell-shaped curve from the Irreplaceables.

The quickest description of a Replacement Level staff member is that if one of them left our school, we could almost certainly do at least as well, and most likely quite a bit better, employing someone else. If your district has even minimal applicants to choose from, you should have no concerns about losing a Replacement Level employee. And, potentially, a Replacement Level could even be such a negative force or hindrance that you would be better off even if you did not hire a replacement at all.

When we address the issue of retaining our existing staff members, we must remember that what we really want to do is retain our *effective* staff members. Losing someone who is not effective is not a negative at all. It is also critical to understand that the Replacement Level person is the least likely staff member to leave voluntarily. Because of whatever limitations they have in interpersonal skills, work ethic, or talents, they have few if any alternative job opportunities. Seldom would they interview well, and if their employers were honest, they would have poor references to assist them. We are not concerned about retaining this level of staff member. Quite the opposite should be the case.

But even within the Replacement Level group there are different characteristics and groups. The Replacement Levels fall into two categories—Harmless and Negative Force. Let's examine each.

The group we call Harmless represents people who are not very good but stop short of being a Negative Force. Their classroom performance seldom triggers parent complaints or office referrals, but it also does little to encourage learning. They contribute little, if anything, of value, but they do not get in the way. We tend to tolerate our Harmless employees; often, they hover just off our radar screen, not drawing attention or raising hackles the way our Negative Forces do. But it may be a misnomer to call these people Harmless; we can't really afford to keep them around. Everyone who works with students in our schools needs to pull a fair share of the weight. Furthermore, sometimes Harmless staff members provide an audience for more vocal negative leaders who would have much less impact without these followers.

The easiest way to describe the Negative Forces is "addition by subtraction." If they left our organization, we would (discreetly) celebrate, because our entire organization would be better off. Just as the WOWs spread positive effects far beyond their classroom, the Negative Forces send out discouraging ripples. This negativity can surface in working with their students, supervising other staff members, or griping in the teachers' workroom. And, unfortunately, it can leave traces on every path they cross.

In addition to the power they personally wield, they often draw others in the school into this dynamic. In an attempt to calm angry fires, administrators may actually protect Replacement Level staff members by reducing their responsibilities—giving them smaller classes, keeping them off committees, and shielding them from extra duties. We must recognize that the more we do this, the less likely they are to leave. And yet if they did leave, we could probably hire someone a great deal better.

Our initial instinct may be to protect our staff members, but we must realize how much better off the students and our schools would be if we improved the quality of our employees. Being aware of who is essential to retain and whom we might benefit from losing can assist in keeping this focus.

These same levels apply to all of our support staff. The lucky ones among us have some secretaries that rank as Irreplaceable. Many of our teaching assistants might be Solids. Perhaps we can name a bus driver or coach at the Replacement Level. We probably all have many people in each of the groupings. By understanding where our current faculty and staff fit into the scale, and by assessing potential replacements, we can recognize where to focus our retention and recruiting efforts. Our organization will be as good as its people.

We Are Not in a Vacuum

As leaders, we may not be able to slot every teacher neatly into one of these six categories—and that's fine. We cannot even do that with people we know. However, this framework should provide some guidelines to use to look at everyone in our schools more objectively. As you know, we can grow fond of people we have worked with for several years, regardless of their abilities. We remember that they sent us flowers when we were in the hospital or started our car every time the temperature dropped below freezing on a snowy afternoon. The relationships people build as they work together make it difficult to think of letting someone go. Of course these things come into play. Yet it is essential that we do not lose sight of our primary focus: What contributions does each person make to our school and our students? Taking the time to individually rank each staff member can help us establish a clearer picture of where to focus our retention efforts. It may also increase our understanding of different types of people, which can strengthen our abilities in selecting new teachers when opportunities arise.

It is also valuable to understand that people are not locked into a category. People grow and change. As leaders, we work to channel that change in the direction of improvement. We would like our best Solids to become Irreplaceable. Even moving someone from Negative Force to Harmless, or Harmless to Solid, can make a big difference. Yet we should not lose sight of the value of talent as an important factor in making the correct decisions. Understanding ability levels can assist us in increasing retention and recruitment efforts.

Weighing the Peripherals

One of the challenges we face in evaluating staff members is that their jobs are so complex. A 10-year veteran teaches 10th-grade mathematics and coaches the girls' softball team. A weaker fourth-grade teacher does a great job coordinating the awards assembly at the end of every year. One of our seventh-grade core team teachers is a single parent who needs the income. All these factors come into our thoughts and emotions, and they should. But all of these aspects are peripheral to the core question: How effective is each teacher in working with students? Although we need to consider the whole person when we make a ranking of the contributions of each staff member, the decisive factor needs to be how well they work with the young people in our schools.

We have an obligation to serve all our employees. All good leaders do. However, a much more essential requirement is to serve our students. Maintaining a focus on our students can enable us to make clear decisions when evaluating our staff members. Although we always want to do what is best for our teachers, we always *must* do what is best for the students.

3

Opportunity Costs

When administrators think about teacher retention, they sometimes focus on the *number* of staff members who return or depart each year rather than on their abilities. In terms of dollars, the cost of having to replace a teacher can be significant. In terms of students, the cost of having to keep a poor teacher can be immeasurable. These two statements are quite obvious. A less obvious factor is related to the question, "What else could I get?" It is impossible to determine the cost or value of retaining a teacher unless you also determine the cost or value of the replacement. In other words, if we lose a great teacher, but we can hire an equally adept educator, then the cost is really only measured in dollars. However, if we lose a great teacher and hire someone less effective, then the cost is financial *and* educational. The converse is also applicable. If we lose an average teacher and hire an Irreplaceable, any financial cost is offset by an educational gain. Understanding this concept is critical in determining the actual cost and practical benefit of staff turnover.

Opportunity Costs

A classic term in economics is *opportunity cost*. Whenever we purchase an item, there are two ways to assess its cost. One is the purchase price: a $50 sweater costs us $50 in funds. But potentially there is another cost—a more significant item that we can no longer purchase because we have spent that $50. For example, we lose the *opportunity* to buy a much nicer $75 sweater when it goes on sale for $50. This is a pretty simple concept, and potentially one that we are already well versed in. When we think of moneys in a school district, opportunity cost always comes into play. For every new teacher we hire, we lose an opportunity to use that money to increase existing personnel salaries. Each time we pay to repair a copier, we reduce the funds available to buy other supplies.

The purpose of discussing opportunity costs is not to engulf us all in buyer's remorse. Instead it is to help us put into perspective the intangibles that come in addition to the straight dollar costs of staff turnover.

My father used to say, "I saved $35 dollars at the store today." When we asked him how, he would reply, "I didn't buy anything." Though this may have been a silly attempt at humor, it reflects the concept of opportunity costs. When we use up a resource, we no longer have the chance to use it again. By the same token, if we can replace a resource with a more valuable one, then we may have increased our net worth rather than diminished it. How does this apply in keeping our best and brightest teachers on board? Let's break the idea of retention down into simple concepts.

What Did We Lose?

The first thing we have to weigh when a staff member leaves our organization is "What did we lose?" Hopefully, the six descriptions of types and values of teachers discussed in the Chapter 2 will provide a little perspective. If we take a list of all staff members in our school or district and objectively place them into groups—Stabilizers, Harmless, WOW—we have a pretty good idea of the cost in terms of talent. We should include the intangibles related to their relationships among the staff, extracurricular responsibilities, and so on. As supervisors, we might also consider how much of our time and energy they take. Are these high-maintenance teachers or low-maintenance teachers?

Providing objectivity in a potentially emotional situation can help us determine whether turnover is a problem to be addressed or a blessing in disguise. Leaders who develop an understanding of the effectiveness of each staff member are better able to determine how to respond to a potential departure.

Determining the value of any staff member we lose is essential. However, we must also ask an equally important second question.

What Else Can We Get?

Assessing the tangible dollar cost of recruiting, hiring, and inducting a staff member may be easy. Establishing the quality of potential replacements is not. In a district that attracts a rich pool of applicants for most positions, we may regularly aim for Irreplaceables and, at a minimum, have the opportunity to choose Solids. If we find ourselves in this fortunate situation, then that helps determine the intangible cost of losing a teacher. If we lose a Solid from our staff, at least we will break even in talent; with luck, we may move up by adding an Irreplaceable. We would still work to retain our quality teachers, especially our WOWs. But losing a Replacement Level staff member would have real value—and our definition of Replacement Level may be broader because we can almost always find someone in the upper echelon of quality.

Other schools and districts may not be quite so fortunate. Board policy or teacher contract rules may stipulate that we can't choose replacements but have to take whatever we get. A school that doesn't enjoy the best reputation may face district candidates or even outside applicants whose quality is not very appealing. In a district that traditionally has a shortage of applicants—particularly talented ones—we may need to broaden our definition of Irreplaceable because we can't be sure to find someone who will be a Solid in another setting. You know your personnel; you must get to know the candidate pool you have to work with. Section IV of this book suggests ways to increase the depth and quality of your candidate pool, but no matter what your circumstances, you need to know the talent level of potential replacement staff members.

What If the Current Staff Were Applicants?

To compare the quality of current staff member with potential applicants, simply think of each of your existing teachers as applicants rather than employees. Then ask yourself these four questions:

1. Would you want to interview this person?
2. After meeting this person, would you be likely to extend an invitation for a second interview?
3. Would you hire this person in your school or district?
4. Would you actively recruit this person for your school or district?

Take a list of all of your employees. Beside each name, put a plus sign each time you answer yes to one of these four questions. This simple process gives you a quick guide to the value of your current employees. A name that doesn't earn at least two pluses represents a person you do not want to retain—a Replacement Level person. A name with three pluses is most likely a Solid—someone you would hire in your setting, and therefore someone you would like to retain. The teachers with four pluses—those you would actively recruit if you had the opportunity—are your Irreplaceables, or at least very capable Solid staff members.

You can also apply this activity to the candidates you are able to attract. If you have a high-quality pool to choose from, you might be willing to hire only the strongest candidates—potential Irreplaceables. Other schools and districts might be elated to attract Solids; at times, they may have to settle for a Harmless applicant. The level of talent available in your pool of applicants makes a difference in your decisions about which staff members you need to retain.

If you have a strong pool of replacements, retaining ineffective teachers carries a high opportunity cost. Losing a good teacher when you have little chance of hiring someone as good also carries an opportunity cost. Any opening on your staff presents an opportunity to hire a WOW. Of course, it also opens the door to employing a Negative Force or a Harmless. Retaining existing staff represents a benefit and a liability. When we hold on to a known quantity (good or bad), we lose the opportunity to choose someone else.

In addition to this one-to-one comparison of departing staff members and their replacements, school leaders must consider other factors in terms of their effects on the school and district.

The Strength of Stability

The loss of a principal can interrupt a school's movement in a positive direction. Sometimes the school's culture is strong enough to keep the momentum going; in other cases, a principal's departure comes as a hard blow. Likewise, at the district level a new superintendent could slow or stall the progress of a productive program or effort. The same struggle can occur within a school when a significant teacher departs.

Teachers lead many of the best movements in a school. Though we would hope to sustain the growth if a teacher leader departed, that might not be realistic because that person may have been the heart of a program. A teacher leading the charge may be an Irreplaceable staff member or one of the Solids. It may be possible to replace that teacher's abilities in the classroom, but a particular focused effort may suffer. Others may attempt to take over guiding the process, but without the originators, their efforts may be futile.

Additionally, gradual attrition can make an overall difference. Perhaps specific training is provided to an entire faculty. As these people leave, the original feeling and flavor of the efforts may drop. The talent may be replaceable, but some of the experience levels may not be.

For example, a junior high school reconfigured as a middle school may have undergone significant staff development regarding interdisciplinary teaming, advisory practices, and flexible block scheduling. Extensive training may have established a rich understanding of these concepts throughout the faculty. As teachers leave, their replacements may be equivalent in general ability but not in the richness of understanding about middle level practices. Although future efforts may increase the knowledge level of new hires, these efforts may not be as involved as previous staff development.

As another example, consider the mission statement of a school or district. Often, the very process of developing this statement constitutes one of its main values. People who were part of the process are much more likely to feel ownership than are staff members who may have been added after the philosophy was put in place. This does not mean that we cannot attempt to establish a parallel understanding, but something may be lacking.

The Value of Experience

Another aspect of teacher retention involves long-term goals and growth. The value of experience may be difficult to measure. Though length of service does not make up for a lack of talent, it can help maximize a teacher's abilities. New staff members can refine their skills as they gather an experiential base. However, frequent turnover in a faculty can interfere with this process.

New teachers bring excitement and energy to a school. This is definitely a positive. But veterans provide stability. The combination of energy and stability sets the stage for both rookies and old hands to realize their potential. This makes retaining high-quality, experienced teachers a key goal for educational organizations, and combining the exuberance of youth with the wisdom of experience is a necessary component of effective leadership. We need to keep our most valuable resources—our best people—as positive role models when we have the opportunity to add new staff. Without a clear understanding of the potential costs of staff turnover, a leader can sometimes lose sight of its benefits.

Section II

Why Teachers Leave

4

From the Mouths of Teachers

Although much of this book is devoted to examining what principals can do to improve teacher retention in their schools, the main focus has been on retaining the *best* teachers in the school. Though a mass exodus of teachers from any school building can have a harmful effect, it is the great teachers whose departure can really hurt a school. Unfortunately, the existing literature on teacher retention and attrition issues fails to differentiate among great teachers, mediocre teachers, and really poor teachers. Nevertheless, it is important for all principals to examine this literature so that they can get a national perception of this issue.

We have known principals who were not remotely affected by issues of teacher retention. These principals were so good, and their staffs so dedicated, that they rarely lost a teacher. Still, they would be well served to understand how big and how real the problems of teacher attrition and the struggles to retain them really are in this country. In the section that follows, we present objective data about how many teachers are leaving the profession. In addition, we explain why these teachers have chosen to leave the profession. All principals need to look at these reasons in light of the situation within their schools. Although the literature summarized next was written by professors, researchers, and project directors, the information that drives it has come from the mouths of teachers themselves. It's important that we all listen to what these teachers have to say.

The Facts about Teacher Retention

The National Center for Education Statistics (1998) predicts that by 2008 approximately 2.4 million teachers will be needed in this country, at a rate of over 200,000 per year (Latham, Gitmer, & Ziomek, 1999). Although the projections can vary somewhat, these numbers are similar to those in many other national reports. Several important factors have contributed to this prediction. First, because of increased birth rates and immigration, student enrollment in American schools is expected to pass 54 million by 2008 (Merrow, 1999; NCES, 1998). Second, more than one-third of the current teaching force is age 50 or older (Recruiting New Teachers, 1998) and therefore likely to retire within the next decade. Third, many national academic reports currently recommend reducing the number of students in each classroom; if schools follow these recommendations, they will need more teachers for these smaller classes (Merrow, 1999; NASBE, 1998).

True, some people consider the main source of the problem to lie in the difficulties in finding and attracting new teachers to the profession. Ingersoll (1998) concludes, however, that it is a mistake to assume that hiring difficulties result from teacher shortages in the conventional sense of the availability of candidates willing to enter the profession. Look at any college of education within the United States and you are likely to find more than enough candidates. The demand for new teachers comes about primarily because teachers choose to leave their jobs at far higher rates than do professionals in many other occupations (NCES, 1998). "We're misdiagnosing the problem as 'recruitment' when it's really 'retention'" (Merrow, 1999, p. 64). There are plenty of candidates out there. Too many of them begin careers as teachers, only to choose a different career within a few short years.

The National Center for Education Statistics (1997) reports that across the nation, 9.3% of public school teachers leave before they complete their first year in the classroom, and over one-fifth of public school teachers leave within their first three years of teaching. This suggests a real lack of mentoring and induction programs designed to help these newcomers become successful, fulfilled teachers. In addition, nearly 30% of teachers leave the profession within five years of entry, and more disadvantaged schools report even higher attrition rates (Darling-Hammond, 1999; Delgado, 1999).

Why Is This Happening?

Although none of this is necessarily startling news, it confirms that many of the behaviors of some of the best principals are clearly implicated in what research has shown about reasons teachers give for remaining in the profession. Researchers have linked a number of aspects of job satisfaction to teacher retention. Among these are administrative leadership and support (Betancourt-Smith, Inman, & Marlow, 1994; Billingsley, 1993) and interaction and emotional support from mentors and colleagues (Billingsley, 1993; Kim & Loadman, 1994). Relationships with parents and families (Billingsley, 1993; Shann, 1998) and with students (Kim & Loadman, 1994; Shann, 1998), as well as opportunities for advancement (Kim & Loadman, 1994), were related to teachers' job satisfaction.

Although teachers may cite salary and family relocation as reasons for leaving a particular school or district, we won't dwell on these factors here—both because the principal has little control over them and because teachers give other more pressing reasons for attrition. Issues in the work environment often provide the impetus for teachers leaving the profession. Futrell (1999) describes the frustration that many teachers feel because of the "rigid, bureaucratic hierarchy in which teachers are treated like tall children rather than like professionals" (p. 31). A lack of authority to make decisions about curriculum, assessment, scheduling, and policy leads both experienced and novice teachers to doubt their professional status. These feelings of doubt are enhanced when teachers feel the pressures of accountability without some degree of buffer from the principal. The best principals provide protection from excessive stress, enabling teachers to do their jobs in a less threatening environment.

Opportunities for further development of professional knowledge and skills are likely essential components in addressing concerns and needs of classroom teachers. Like other professionals, teachers feel more fulfilled in their work if they believe the work environment provides opportunities for their continued growth and development. Likewise, among the goals for educational reform developed by the Holmes

Group (1986) is a stated focus on recognizing differences in teachers' knowledge, skill, and commitment in their education, certification, and work (p. 4).

Many first-year teachers report that they experience overwhelming isolation as they leave the support of student-teaching cohorts, cooperating teachers, and university supervisors that the preparation phase provided to them. Leaving this familiar support may shatter the goals, diminish the spirits, and destroy the self-confidence of first-year teachers (Delgado, 1999). Principals must be aware of this, and they must provide opportunities for mentoring and developing first-year teachers without overwhelming them.

Support for teachers, however, must extend beyond their first years in the classroom. Continuous dialogue with colleagues and professional studies are needed throughout teachers' careers and should be an important part of each school day (NASBE, 1998). Such activity will equip teachers to lead reforms within their schools and to build the status of the profession. Many school districts have developed programs for supporting and evaluating experienced teachers similar to those for new teachers. When teachers have difficulty meeting set standards, peer review and intensive support and assistance help them to either improve their practices or leave the field.

A Culture of Support

Section III focuses on how principals can create the kind of culture where teachers can thrive and remain motivated and fulfilled. Both authors have extensive experience studying schools and helping to improve their cultures, so the issue of creating a positive school culture is a natural point of discussion. Much of the literature on teacher retention and school environment focuses primarily on school climate—the visible aspect of school culture—rather than on school culture itself. Although the two terms are related, it is the culture of a school that determines the collective beliefs, values, mores, and ethos of the professional staff. It is through enhancing the culture of schools, therefore, that principals can make the greatest impact in improving environmental factors for teachers.

Although studies most often look at school climate, some studies address school culture specifically. According to Stolp (1994), a school's culture correlates with teachers' attitudes toward work. Schools with stronger cultures have more motivated teachers (Cheng, 1993, cited in Stolp, 1994). The environments of schools with positive cultures often possess strong organizational ideology, shared participation, charismatic leadership, and intimacy. Stolp contends that these factors cause teachers to have higher job satisfaction and increased productivity.

An investigation of school culture led by Israeli researcher Isaac Friedman (1991) looked at its relationship to teacher burnout. Friedman's study not only found that organizational variables such as school culture and climate make a difference but also revealed four school culture variables that lead to teacher burnout: having achievement behavior set by administrators, inadequate level of trust with teachers' professionalism, "circumscribing" school culture, and poor physical environment. Many previous studies have concluded that, in the majority of cases, the cause for burnout is environment (Cherniss, 1980; Etzion, Kafry, & Pines, 1982; Friedman & Lotan, 1985; Kahn, 1975; Maslach, 1982; Pines, Aronson, & Kafry 1981; Shirom, 1987, cited in Friedman, 1991). Other findings from studies of teacher burnout reveal characteristics of high- and low-burnout schools. In high-burnout schools, teachers do not operate as a team, teachers rarely serve on committees together, and the physical environment is more sterile. In low-burnout schools, the organizational culture is more flexible, duties for positions change over time, and socializing among teachers is more evident. Therefore, positive cultural elements in a school could affect teacher burnout rates and, ultimately, retention.

Also closely related to an investigation of school culture and teacher retention is a study by Chittom & Sistrunk (1990) that looked solely at the relationship between school culture and teacher satisfaction. The results showed a significant relationship between respondents' perceptions of school culture and teacher satisfaction; the higher the score on job satisfaction, the better the teacher's impression of the school's culture. These data support previous findings (Sistrunk, 1982, cited in Chittom & Sistrunk, 1990) that job satisfaction is related to supervisory behavior but not to the subject a teacher teaches. In addition, a significant correlation between positive perceptions of school culture and positive perceptions of principal behavior was found. This concept was expanded on in research by Whitaker (1997) and Fiore (1999).

Perhaps the most significant study for research on teacher retention and school culture is Weiss's (1999) investigation of teachers' plans to remain in the profession. Findings reveal that a school culture that includes strong collaboration and teacher decision making most strongly correlates to high morale, stronger commitment to teaching, and intentions to remain in teaching. This study indicates that the higher the school culture is rated, the higher is the level of planned retention. There are four factors acknowledged for helping to retain teachers, the largest being "perceptions of school social organization and climate factors" (p. 865). The most important finding is described as follows:

> First-year teachers' perceptions of school leadership and culture and teacher autonomy and discretion shape the extent of their willingness to do their best work, to commit to teaching as a career choice again, and to plan to stay in teaching. (p. 869)

It's All in the Atmosphere

Clearly, teachers give many reasons for leaving the teaching profession. Some of these reasons are so far outside the principal's control that they are simply not worth discussing. However, it is those reasons (salary, relocation) that seem to garner the most attention. It causes us to wonder sometimes if people really want solutions or if they are content to identify problems that can't be solved. From the principal's perspective, low teacher salary is a problem that can't be solved.

The good news is that if we listen to teachers, we discover that the vast majority of them are leaving for other reasons.

These teachers are leaving the profession, or at least contemplating leaving it, because of environmental reasons, such as feelings among colleagues, support from administrators, and relationships with parents. These are issues that principals can deal with, and the best ones do so on a regular basis. Most of the remainder of this book is devoted to helping you understand specifically how to overcome these environmental issues. One key component is assistance for creating an atmosphere that makes teaching rewarding. First, however, we need to return our focus to the great teachers. Although teacher attrition is a national concern, the real issue is retaining the great ones. Chapter 5 helps to ensure that we keep focusing our efforts on the best teachers in our schools.

5

Are We Talking about the Great Ones?

Now that we have seen what recent research tells us about the reasons teachers leave the profession, we can turn our attention to the real issue. Although it is important for all educators to understand the reasons teachers cite for leaving, we all must admit that some of our teachers ought to leave the profession. We cannot continue thinking that all instances of teacher attrition are bad, or that we must retain all teachers. In reality, it is only the great teachers in our schools whose retention concerns us. We need to make sure that we are talking about the great ones.

When the best teachers are asked to describe those elements of their jobs that lead to the greatest feelings of satisfaction, invariably they speak of administrative support, cooperative leadership, and an understanding and approachable principal. When probed to explain what they mean, the greatest of our teachers generally reply that their satisfaction comes less from the leader's personality as such than from how the leader makes them feel. As an illustration, consider that many of the studies cited in Chapter 4 demonstrated that feeling respected and appreciated made a big difference in teachers' decisions about whether to stay at a given school. These themes, admittedly quite predictable, are also consistent with the findings of Frederick Herzberg, as described in his *Hygiene-Motivation Theory*. Herzberg conducted his research and developed this widely used motivational theory during the 1950s and 1960s in an industrial, not an educational, environment. Throughout his research, Herzberg found that certain factors tended to cause a worker to feel unsatisfied with his or her job. These factors seemed to directly relate to the employee's environment such as the physical surroundings, supervisors, and even the company itself. Herzberg developed the Hygiene-Motivation Theory based on this observation.

According to this theory, for a worker to be happy and therefore productive, these environmental factors must not cause discomfort. Although the elimination of the environmental problems may make a worker productive, Herzberg discovered that it would not necessarily motivate him. So, the question remained, "How can leaders *motivate* employees?" Many school principals believe that motivating employees requires giving rewards. Herzberg, however, believed that the workers get motivated through feeling responsible for and connected to their work. In this case, the work itself is rewarding. Leaders, it has been shown, can help employees connect to their work by giving them more authority over the job, as well as by offering direct and individual feedback. Herzberg's research proved that people will strive to achieve what he calls hygiene needs because they are unhappy without them; but once satisfied, the effect soon wears off—satisfaction is temporary. *Hygiene needs* in the workplace include policy, relationship with supervisor, work conditions, salary, company car, status, security, relationship with subordinates, and personal life. True motivators, on the other hand, were found to be other completely different factors: achievement, recognition, the work itself, responsibility, advancement, and personal growth (See Figure 5.1).

Figure 5.1. Herzberg's Motivators and Hygiene Factors.

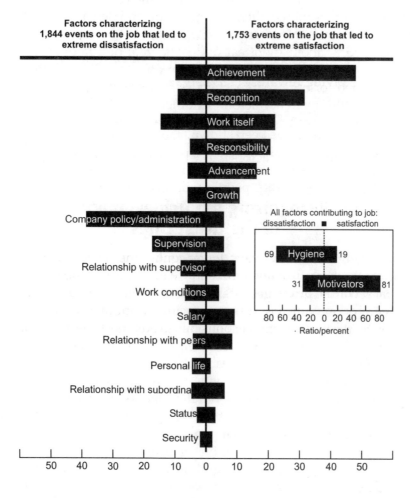

When you consider Herzberg's theory in relation to teachers and schools, it becomes pretty difficult to argue against his results. Sure, certain teachers will claim that money and working conditions are motivators for them, but are these teachers the great ones we need to focus on? We can all think of people who defy Herzberg's results and the conventional wisdom; should we strive to retain these teachers? Is it for the salvation of these folks that this book is written?

The answer to all three of these questions is an emphatic
no. The great teachers that we need to focus our energies on
are the very people for whom achievement, recognition, the
work itself, responsibility, advancement, and personal growth
are motivators. Herzberg got it right; at least he did when we
are talking about the great ones. The goal of school leaders
must, therefore, be to enhance the motivators that Herzberg
identified for our great teachers while decreasing the annoy-
ance of the hygiene factors. In other words, school leaders
need to manage hygiene factors like salary and working conditions, but they need to focus the bulk of their leadership efforts on motivating factors like achievement, recognition, and
personal growth.

Recognizing the Achievement of the Great Ones

There are many ways to recognize the achievement of
great teachers. Whatever method we use—positive notes, special rewards, privileges, praise before superiors, or any number of other methods—it is vitally important that we remember to recognize achievements whenever possible with our
best teachers. Although all teachers can be motivated through
recognition, it is our best teachers who most often do things
worthy of recognition. In giving this recognition to teachers,
we do need to be cautious about the benefits and potential pitfalls of public praising, so that we can best decide whether
their recognition should happen publicly or privately.

Ben Bissell (1992) mentions five important components
that make praise and recognition effective. He states that
praise works best when it is *authentic, specific, immediate, clean,*
and *private.* Principals should, therefore, always ensure that
their praise is authentic and for a very specific purpose (e.g.,
specific student achievement). To maximize opportunities for
immediate recognition, principals should be visible (more on
this in later chapters). Visibility only enhances one's ability to
praise immediately, because it puts the principal right there
when positive behavior occurs. Clean praise is, of course, important because it comes without conditions or strings at-

tached. When we attach conditions to praise or recognition, the motivating power that Herzberg describes is lost.

The issue of keeping praise private is a more contentious one. We agree that, when you are in doubt, it is always safest to praise somebody in private. Public praising, after all, can be embarrassing and can cause hard feelings. However, there must be occasions when public praising is most appropriate. After all, it's the public element of praise that transforms the praise into recognition. Public praise gives you a vehicle to teachable moments, and it allows the influence of the teacher being praised to reach many other teachers.

The principal needs to use judgment in determining when to praise in private and when to do so in public. A good rule of thumb is to remember that most praise is safest in private, but that there are times when the public element of the praise will give the teacher the level of recognition that is truly motivational. There will also be times where the act being praised is one that everybody should know about for maximum benefit to the school.

Assisting Great Teachers in Personal and Professional Growth

The best teachers in our school, the ones we want to retain at all costs, are also the teachers who are most likely to be concerned with continuous improvement. Every principal has recognized the irony of this. In many schools, teachers are asked to set goals at the beginning of the year. The less effective teachers tend to choose simple, vague goals: "I want to enhance my classroom management." Such goals are not only vague but also difficult to measure. How, for example, does one measure "enhance"? School leaders, therefore, need to help less effective teachers write goals that will actually have meaning.

The best teachers in the school tend to write the most ambitious goals: "I want to develop a strategy that will improve reading comprehension for the students in the lowest quartile." They then tend to ask for assistance in gathering the data to identify students, and more often than not, they appreciate feedback as they develop new strategies. If your school has teachers with this degree of professionalism and with this much desire to improve, then you must take seriously your responsibility to help them. If you don't support ambitious teachers like these, they are far more likely to lose their motivation and seek employment elsewhere.

Principals must constantly focus on the personal and professional growth that great teachers want. One excellent way to show your support is to keep your eyes and ears open for workshops, conferences, and other development opportunities that might benefit these teachers. No matter how small your budget, set aside funds for teachers to attend these staff development opportunities.

John Seyfarth (2002) discusses boredom as a major source of teacher dissatisfaction. This is particularly so for great teachers who are not afforded the opportunity to enhance their work by learning and trying something new. Less effective teachers tend not to suffer from boredom because they have yet to master their craft. This is obviously not the case with our most effective teachers. Seyfarth states:

> Administrators can help relieve boredom by providing stimulating staff development programs, providing for conference travel and sabbatical leave, and arranging transfers to new situations for teachers who request them. (Seyfarth, 2002, p. 97)

It's imperative for school leaders to recognize the need great teachers have for continuous growth. This is not to imply that the same need should be ignored in other teachers. All teachers should be provided with ample opportunities to grow personally and professionally. We focus on the great ones because they are the ones we most want to retain and the ones who are most interested in continuous growth.

Section III

Creating, Fostering, and Sustaining Quality

6

Building a
Quality Culture

Section III illuminates the importance of creating environments, belief systems, norms, and an ethos that support quality teaching and make it safe and comfortable for teachers to remain working in their school. Although it is vitally important to know the differences between quality teachers and the rest (as discussed in Part I of this book), it is equally important for us to understand our role in creating the kind of culture that supports our quality teachers and helps them to understand their value.

In Chapter 1 we established the relationship between our teachers' self-concepts and the self-concepts of our students. This is an important relationship to understand. Because students' self-concepts have repeatedly been linked to their levels of achievement, this is a concept that ought to be of great concern to all school leaders. However, a principal leading a school with 2,000 students, or even one with 300 students, will find it challenging at best to have a direct, positive impact on their self-concepts. Working on improving the self-concepts of the school faculty is a much more manageable task. And, because our positive self-concepts will ultimately trickle down to the students, this is a great place to start building our school's culture.

A Culture That Feels Good

The term *school culture* describes the guiding belief system, norms, values, ethos, and resulting feelings that propel stakeholders to act in a certain way within the organization. In some schools, the culture is so positive that faculty members would never dream of griping about a student's inability to learn or a parent's lack of support. In these schools, the words *accountability* and *assessment* don't trigger a sense of doom and gloom. Principals are valued and held in high regard, and teachers realize that they are the most important adults in the school. These schools *feel good;* because of that feeling, students like learning, teachers like teaching, and parents support both learners and teachers.

Other schools have a less positive culture. Teachers gripe about administrators; administrators, about parents; parents, about teachers; teachers, about students—and the spiral continues. The words *assessments* and *accountability* loom as dark clouds overhead. These schools *don't feel good.* As a result, students resist learning, teachers resent teaching, and parents offer little in the way of support.

It is obvious that the Irreplaceable parts in our schools—the teachers we most need to protect—will be much less apt to consider leaving a school with a positive culture. It is also obvious that the high degree of professionalism characteristic of these teachers takes quite a blow where the culture is negative. Therefore, all principals must recognize the power of a positive school culture and do all that they can to create, foster, and sustain positive cultures. Although some elements are beyond the principal's control, research and practice have identified many leadership behaviors that will improve the culture of a school or sustain an already positive one. In this chapter, we list some steps you can take, regardless of the demographic characteristics of your school, to promote a positive school culture. If you exhibit as many of these behaviors as you possibly can, you will increase the likelihood that your school's culture will *feel good.*

What Should I Do?

In studying the behaviors of principals who were leading schools with extremely powerful cultures, the following list emerged. Specifically, the list grew out of conversations with teachers as they attempted to explain what their principal did or failed to do to impact the culture of their school. These 10 behaviors are summarized to help all principals understand how they can most readily and easily have a positive impact on the culture of their school. This list, in slightly greater detail, was originally presented in *Creating Connections for Better Schools: How Leaders Enhance School Culture* (Fiore, 2001).

1. *Be visible to all school stakeholders.* Studies have shown that school leaders who are visible to stakeholders help create and foster positive school cultures (Fiore, 1999). This is largely a result of the feelings of comfort reported when the principal is visible regularly and in various settings. In addition, visibility—exhibited through behaviors such as "management by walking around"—makes the management tasks of school leaders easier to accomplish (Frase & Melton, 1992), because their presence will inhibit some negative behaviors.

2. *Communicate regularly and purposefully.* The best school leaders use varied forms of communication to provide feedback regularly to all stakeholders. Visibility makes this easier and more natural. It is important that this communication occurs in good times as well as in bad times, so that people don't feel apprehensive when the principal approaches them. Instead, students, faculty, and parents understand that the principal communicates both positive and negative news.

3. *Never forget that principals are role models.* Principals must recognize that they are the most influential people in a school system. Teachers, staff, parents, students, and community members *do* look to the school leaders as role models. With this in mind, principals should model behaviors consistent with the sustenance of a positive school culture. These behaviors, in addition to the others enumerated in this list, include optimism and enthusiasm.

4. *Be passionate about your work.* The most effective school leaders seem to love their jobs. They have a passion for schools and a passion for leadership that their followers can clearly witness. The imperative for all school leaders is to become more passionate about their work and clearer about

what they hope to accomplish (Greenfield, 1985). This may be a difficult goal, for passion comes from within and is difficult to copy.

5. *Understand how responsible you are for the culture.* The best school leaders believe that they are responsible for virtually everything that happens in their schools. The most effective principals realize their responsibility to protect the needs and integrity of the entire school community (Sergiovanni, 1996). They do not "pass the buck" and blame others for problems in the school. These principals, instead, are highly proactive leaders.

6. *Keep yourself organized.* Disorganized administrators find time management burdensome. School administrators who are organized can more easily carve out time for instructional leadership, school–community relations, and personnel management. Studies have shown that stakeholders appreciate and rely on the organization of their leader (Whitaker, 1997; Fiore, 1999). Principals for whom organization doesn't come naturally must surround themselves with office staff who can assist in this regard. In other words, they must find ways to manage this weakness.

7. *Exhibit a positive outlook.* As role models, the best school administrators realize that attitudes are, indeed, contagious. To create and sustain a positive school culture, school leaders must consistently radiate positive energy. They must proactively approach their work, never forgetting the mission of the school. Furthermore, effective principals strengthen the culture of their schools by ensuring that the entire school community shares its mission and vision (Buell, 1992).

8. *Take pride in your school's physical appearance.* When the school environment looks neat, attractive, and inviting, then students feel engaged and teachers are inspired. Therefore, effective leaders recognize

the importance of enhancing and maintaining their school's appearance. More significantly, they do not leave this to chance—or even to the custodial and maintenance staff. Rather, they take responsibility for making this a priority and following through.

9. *Empower others appropriately.* Our schools need leaders who understand when and how to empower others to share leadership. They realize that people need a stake in the outcome of an event and the capacity to lead before they can be empowered. These leaders recognize that power, like love, multiplies when it is shared with others. They appropriately empower teachers, support staff, students, and parents.

10. *Demonstrate stewardship.* School leaders who understand their roles as stewards of the community are inspiring to followers. Effective administrators exercise stewardship when they commit themselves to serving, caring for, and protecting their schools and their stakeholders (Sergiovanni, 1996). Principals need to make the choice to serve their school first. Without making such a choice, a principal's capacity to lead is profoundly limited (Greenleaf, 1977).

Principals who understand the importance of these 10 behaviors and try to exhibit them as often as possible can use their tremendous influence as culture builders to create environments where teachers can flourish. This is not to imply that all teachers will flourish if principals exhibit these behaviors—but it will make a difference to the teachers who matter most. Although the main purpose for developing a positive school culture is to assist in student learning and development, another important reason for doing so is that positive teachers enjoy working in a positive school. We owe it to our students to create an environment where our best teachers will want to stay.

Improving Classroom Culture
by Improving School Culture

Another reason why school leaders must focus on building a quality school culture is the powerful effect this can have on building quality classroom cultures. Our Irreplaceable teachers have already developed quality cultures in their classrooms, but we can indirectly assist them by improving the cultures in our Solids' classrooms. This, in turn, carries two distinct benefits. First, it nudges these teachers a bit closer to the category of Irreplaceable. Second, because the Irreplaceable is likely to share students with some of the Solids (if not this year, then next), we set these students up for a better overall educational experience than they would have had otherwise. But how do we do it? How do we upgrade the classroom culture of our Solid teachers without spending all day in their classrooms?

The answer lies in our success at modeling the kind of culture we expect. By adhering to the behaviors listed earlier and supplementing these with behaviors that boost morale in your particular school, you will consistently model appropriate behaviors. This, in turn, will make it easier to expect similar behavior from your teachers, particularly your Solids. Even if your positive behavior is only infectious enough to change the culture in one classroom, think of the potential impact on the students in that classroom. Then think of how this may raise the spirits and performance of that one Solid classroom teacher. Finally, consider that your Irreplaceables, those teachers you most want to retain forever, may notice the improvement and feel even better about the overall culture of your school—their school.

Modeling a quality culture does not need to radically change the way you do business. Many principals, after an honest self-examination, have found it easy to get out of the office more and be visible to all school stakeholders. Similarly, principals have focused on their communication and worked to make it more regular, purposeful, and positive. These changes are simple to make. To strengthen their effectiveness, though, it's helpful to throw in a little bit of fun.

Go Fish

At the time of this book's publication, millions of people have already read the groundbreaking book, *Fish! Catch the Energy, Release the Potential*, by Stephen C. Lundin, Harry Paul, and John Christensen. This bestseller, written about Seattle's World Famous Pike Place Fish Market, illustrates that work can be fun and inspiring for anybody. Without giving away too much about *Fish!*, we can say that the book essentially discusses four aspects of the *Fish!* philosophy.

1. *Play*. There should be times at work for a little bit of play. Schools with great cultures experience play on a regular basis. Whether the play takes the form of fun classroom activities or is limited to friendly teachers' lounge banter, taking some time to play will make work more fun and can improve the overall school culture.

2. *Make their day*. The workers at Seattle's World Famous Pike Place Fish Market work hard to make their customers' day. These workers understand that if customers have fun and enjoy coming to the fish market, they will be more likely to return. We can do this in our schools. The best school leaders improve their school's culture daily by making sure their school is a place where all stakeholders (staff, students, parents, community members) enjoy spending time.

3. *Be there*. Being there for people is very much what the 10 behaviors listed earlier in this chapter were about. Great communicators are present with people when they are speaking with them. They don't listen halfway. School culture is improved and teachers feel more appreciated when the principal knows how to be there and give undivided, caring attention.

4. *Choose your attitude*. This is perhaps the most important aspect of the *Fish!* philosophy. Principals need to be reminded that we choose our own atti-

tudes. The principals who do the best job at making teaching rewarding are the principals who choose to have a positive attitude each and every day at work. In time, this positive attitude rubs off on others. Soon, the entire faculty can choose to have a positive attitude each and every day.

The school principal has the power to build a quality culture at school. Failing to recognize this is shirking an essential responsibility. Whether they subscribe to the *Fish!* philosophy or simply live out the 10 key behaviors mentioned earlier, school leaders should realize the value of building a quality culture. The research on teacher retention is clear. When school leaders build great cultures, and when they work hard to make teaching rewarding, as discussed in the Chapter 7, they simply don't have as many concerns about teacher retention as if they ignore these things.

7

Making Teaching Rewarding

Ask a group of teachers the following question: "How many of you could earn more money next year by working in a different occupation?" You are likely to see more hands go up than not; most teachers recognize that their intelligence, specialized skills, and college degrees could open doors to other careers that pay higher salaries. They knew this when they decided to become teachers, and they are reminded of it as they grow in their profession and interact with people in other fields. Yet the vast majority of these educators stay in the teaching profession anyway. Why? What is it about teaching that leads so many intelligent, capable people to settle for a lower salary than they could get elsewhere? What are the other, perhaps less obvious, rewards of the teaching profession? How can we keep the best teachers focused on the value of these other rewards, both intrinsic and extrinsic? In this chapter, we attempt to answer these questions.

Cynics would answer that it is the long vacations and summers off that make the teaching profession so attractive. We know that's not it, though. There simply are rewards to teaching that one cannot get in any other profession. There is a great sense of satisfaction that comes from helping young people succeed. There is a sense of achievement and accomplishment that one feels after igniting a spark of curiosity in a child. Finally, there are immeasurable rewards that grow out of knowing that you have made a real difference in the life of a child. Every school leader has a responsibility to keep teachers mindful of these facts. Every school leader must always strive to make teaching the rewarding occupation it can be.

If You Don't Have
Something Nice to Say...

When we were kids, our mothers would say, "If you don't have something nice to say to somebody, then don't say anything at all." It's funny how Mom's wisdom still rings true today. For principals, this statement is a good reminder that we should think twice about the negative or "constructive" things that we say and concentrate on delivering positive messages to teachers. This is not to imply that we should never offer constructive criticism or even a straightforward reprimand, if the situation warrants. Instead, the message here is to focus less on these negative interactions and more on the positive interactions that we can have with teachers. There are several reasons why this is so.

First, our Irreplaceable teachers need this positive feedback. As motivational theories continuously show, people thrive on positive feedback. This is not to say that Irreplaceables should never be corrected or assisted if they make errors. The important thing is to provide theses valuable teachers with positive feedback as often as possible so that their own emotional needs can be met. The Irreplaceable teachers make it easy for us to catch them doing something right—they do positive things on a regular, consistent basis.

Too many principals let themselves get so bogged down in the administrative demands of the job, in managing buildings and facilities, that the human elements of leadership suffer. This process is not easy to reverse, particularly in light of the accountability demands placed on contemporary principals. However, principals who are not maximizing their human relations skills must at least give this area greater attention. As Section II of this book indicated, teachers consistently cite the sense that administrators are not supportive as one reason for leaving the profession. The sad reality is that many of these "unsupportive" administrators are, in fact, very supportive. They simply have not done a good enough job of making teachers *feel* supported. It is the *feeling of support* that teachers really crave.

Perception Is Reality

A difficult truth for many principals to accept is that perception is reality. This is particularly so in light of the fact that principals work with so many different stakeholder groups—teachers, parents, and students. If all of these people perceive things differently, than how can perception really be reality? The answer lies in our understanding of what this statement really means.

Saying that "perception is reality" is different from saying that "perception is truth." If two people are debating baseball teams, for example, and one believes that the Atlanta Braves are the best team in baseball, whereas the other maintains that the St. Louis Cardinals are the best, neither of them is necessarily correct or incorrect. Sure, we could look at the current win–loss records of both teams, but would that really indicate which team was best? Not necessarily. Perhaps they have played against different teams. The team with the best winning percentage does not always win the World Series.

Applying "perception is reality" to this debate simply leads us to understand that these two people see things differently. The same thing happens when we look at politics. Although baseball is a much safer analogy, we all know that this country is filled with individuals who see the same political situations differently. When we acknowledge that perception is reality, the only concession we are making is that to any given individual, their personal perception is what they believe to be reality. We gain nothing by flatly telling people that their perceptions are wrong. Unless we have a strong influence on how these people think, we have little chance of altering their perceptions by edict. We gain a great deal, however, by accepting that they see things a certain way and then by carefully, deliberately, and slowly working to help them see that the truth might be slightly different from what they perceive.

Too many school leaders flatly deny that a teacher's perception of poor administrative support could have any merit. We all know people who, when criticized, immediately begin discrediting the critic's perceptions. Even if a principal can point to solid evidence of supportive behavior, it is far wiser to acknowledge that the teacher's contrary perception is that teacher's reality. The best principals know that discrediting or rejecting that perception will not change it. Instead, they set to work to create a different impression.

Didn't I Just See You?

One of the easiest ways for principals to become aware of teachers' perceptions regarding support is to be visible as often as possible. Visibility, in this case, means more than just standing outside of the office so that people who pass by can see you. The best principals are visible to teachers throughout the school day. They visit classrooms; they are accessible before and after school; they regularly spend time where teachers gather socially (break rooms, lounges). We have known principals who actually blocked time in their calendars each day to make this visibility happen, and we have known others who just made it a priority without formally scheduling it. No matter how principals make this happen, what is important is that teachers see principals often, and that principals communicate with teachers during these visits. As we stated in Chapter 6, this visibility will go very far in improving the overall culture of the school as well.

One excellent time for intentional visibility is in the morning before students arrive. As teachers are getting organized for the day, a principal is well served to walk the halls and stop by every room with a teacher in it. These visits needn't last long or intrude on the teachers' preparation time. Rather, they should be brief, sincere opportunities for the principal to check with teachers and ensure that their needs are met. The encounter starts with "Good morning, Jane. How are you doing today?" and moves to comments like these:

- ♦ "Let's hope Billy has a better day. If you need to involve me at any point, remember that I'm just down the hall."

- ♦ "Great work with Juan yesterday. I'm sure you're very proud of the progress he's making. I really want to thank you for all you do for kids."

- ◆ "Have you heard back from Mr. Albertson? You've been handling the situation with his daughter so well. Let me know if you need any additional support from me."

- ◆ "I'm just reminding everybody that we have that assembly at 1:00 today. Have a great day."

What is actually said during these brief visits is not nearly as important as the symbolism behind the regular opportunities to demonstrate your presence and your support. Therefore, it is important to keep the content positive. That doesn't mean that you must exclude any mention of a situation that the teacher might interpret as negative. But you need to be sure that the visits contain positive affirmations and statements of support as often as possible. Also, they must take place regularly, so that teachers will come to expect them and rely on them.

Although the preceding example takes place in the morning before students arrive, these visits can be effective at virtually any time of day that does not intrude on the teacher's important instructional work. Teachers will not feel supported if they believe that the principal is preventing them from getting their work done. Remember, perception is reality.

But I Don't Have Time

Some principals may feel that this degree of visibility will take them away from other necessary tasks. As Stephen Covey says, "Things that matter the most must never be at the mercy of things that matter the least." It is hard to imagine many things as important as helping our best teachers feel supported. That's the main reason for making these visits anyway. However, it is also true that these visits save time in the long run. Many questions that teachers were going to come and ask the principal later or send via e-mail after the school day is over are asked and resolved during these visits. Plus, because resolution of these questions came at your initiative instead of the teachers', the level of support that teachers feel from the principal is that much greater.

Although it is certainly true that some schools are too large to make these daily visits practical, they can be divided and rotated among all of the building administrators. This way, although teachers may not have a conversation with each administrator each day, they will speak with at least one, and, in time, they will have been visited by all administrators.

Making it OK to Care

Support from administrators, which teachers say helps keep them in the profession, is one way to make teaching rewarding without spending money. But the teaching profession offers a host of other rewards that money just can't buy. Most of them are related to school culture, to working in an environment of shared values, happiness, and optimism.

Have you ever noticed that in some schools, it is just cool to care about kids and their education? In these schools, all staff members buy into and feel they are an integral part of the school's mission. It takes work to achieve this mission, but they consider this an enjoyable labor of love. In other schools, caring about education is frowned upon. These schools offer somewhat dreary environments, where staff members feel underappreciated, devalued, and in competition with their colleagues. In these schools, apathy seems safer than caring. An apathetic attitude lowers expectations to reduce the risk that teachers will fall short of meeting them.

That is why principals must help to create, foster, and sustain quality. Just as a plant may suffocate in a dark closet, our Irreplaceable teachers languish in an environment where negativity rules. But in a school where the prevailing attitude is that it's cool to care, the environment nourishes these teachers. As a principal, you must not let the perception be that the teachers with negative attitudes, the teachers who don't seem to care, and the staff members who consistently underperform get the bulk of your attention. You must give your attention to the best teachers, and you must strive to show them that it is indeed OK to care.

Something Positive in My Mailbox?

Originally conceived by Todd Whitaker and mentioned in previous books by both authors, the *Friday Focus* is one of the best ways to positively contribute to a school's culture, communicate important things to faculty members, and consistently pay attention and tribute to your best teachers. The *Friday Focus*, a weekly memo placed in all teachers' mailboxes before they arrive at school on Friday mornings, is designed with the following goals in mind:

◆ As an efficient channel of information, it should communicate important logistical information about upcoming events in the school. This frees up time at staff meetings for a more productive focus on professional development.

◆ As a staff development or inservice tool, it should keep the school's beliefs and vision always front and center.

◆ As a motivational tool, it should mention good, positive things happening in the school and in individual classrooms. This is especially valuable because it provides an opportunity to recognize those outstanding teachers who make great things happen with kids. This recognition will matter to them and will contribute to a feeling that teaching is rewarding.

◆ As a planning aid, the *Friday Focus* contains important logistical information to help staff members organize and prepare for upcoming events.

In short, the *Friday Focus* is an excellent tool for making it cool to care. Although the memo does not increase teachers' salaries or create a way to stay at a school after a spouse has been relocated, it clearly is a valuable tool in retaining the best teachers. The motivational nature of the *Friday Focus*, coupled with the fact that it is presented every week, make it a tool that teachers, particularly the best ones, will really look forward to reading.

8

Keeping the Great Ones Motivated

Motivation is such a powerful force. Without motivation, a person's will to perform a task suffers greatly. We see this in the world of sports, we see it in artistic endeavors, and we see it in our personal lives. It is a tragedy whenever we see somebody with tremendous talent who, for one reason or another, fails to find a once exciting, challenging, and rewarding task to be motivating any longer.

One of the best-known motivational theories is Frederick Herzberg's Hygiene-Motivation Theory (discussed in greater detail in Chapter 5). Also called the *dual factor theory*, this motivational theory recognizes that certain elements of the work environment are motivating, or satisfying to workers, whereas others cause dissatisfaction but do not really motivate people. Among the factors that do lead to satisfaction and a sense of motivation among workers are recognition and accomplishments. It stands to reason, therefore, that principals should do everything possible to recognize the accomplishments of teachers, while also putting teachers in a position that will lead to greater feelings of accomplishment.

Another well-known motivational theory is Abraham Maslow's *hierarchy of needs*. Essentially, Maslow claims that people's needs can be arranged in a hierarchy and that lower-level needs must be satisfied before higher-level needs can become motivating.

As shown in Figure 8.1, according to Maslow, the most basic needs are physiological needs. An individual must have food, water, shelter, clothing, and the like, before higher-level needs such as safety and relationships can be motivating.

Figure 8.1. Maslow's Hierarchy of Need.

It follows logically that the best teachers have had their lower-level needs met and are striving for self-actualization, or at least are close to the top of Maslow's hierarchy. These teachers are motivated by being the best that they can possibly be in everything that they do. Principals who are aware of this continuously challenge these teachers while providing them with praise and recognition to remain motivated.

So, in light of these motivational theories, what specific steps should principals take to keep teachers, particularly the great ones, motivated? It is in this answer that we discover how to keep teaching rewarding. Here we must remember to focus our greatest efforts on keeping our best teachers motivated. Although we certainly want the entire staff to come to work motivated, excited, and engaged every day, we really want to assist those teachers who are striving toward self-actualization with the desire to be all that they can be. These teachers are already making a significant impact on learning for all students. Enhancing their motivation can lead to incredible improvements in the entire school.

Now, we will also devote some energy to motivating our Solids. Remember, these teachers do a reasonably good job with their students. If principals work at motivating these teachers, they may well manage to enhance their abilities and their efforts. Although Solids are good members of our teaching staff, the possibility that we can transform them into Irreplaceables, or at least that they can approximate Irreplaceables, is reason enough to try and keep them motivated.

We shouldn't ignore the Replacement Level teachers, but neither should we waste too much time and effort trying to motivate them. Although it is never a good idea to intentionally lower the motivation of a Replacement Level teacher, we need to realistically understand that efforts at motivating them will likely be unsuccessful. Plus, although this book is about teacher retention in some ways, it is specifically about retaining *quality* teachers. Even a motivated Replacement Level teacher likely will not have a positive impact on student learning. We're better off replacing these people with a Solid teacher and then working on motivating the Solid.

Can I Motivate from the Outside?

Many people think of motivation as an internal process. Because of this, they mistakenly believe that we cannot motivate another person; we can only help them to find their own motivation. Although it's true that being motivated through some internal or intrinsic need fulfillment is lasting, people can also be motivated externally, or by other people. Principals, in particular, need to understand this. We all need to understand that there are things we can do within our schools that will lead to motivation.

Before looking at some specific tips for motivating teachers, consider what Stacy Adams explains in his *Equity Theory of Motivation*. According to Adams, people tend to compare the treatment they receive with the treatment other people receive. Usually, we can identify and compare ourselves to a "comparison other." If we perceive this comparison other to be getting better treatment than we get even though we are doing the same quality work, then we perceive an inequity. Adams describes several ways in which we can restore equity in these situations:

♦ To restore equity, some people do less work. "If I'm not going to be recognized for working hard, I'll simply do less work."

♦ Sometimes people restore equity by switching to a different comparison other. "If I compare myself to somebody else, maybe I'll be happy about the treatment I'm receiving."

♦ Still others attempt to change the work of the comparison other. They simply make the comparison other do poorer work. We see this manifested in negative schools when some teachers corner the enthusiastic new teachers and convince them that enthusiasm does not belong in their school.

♦ A related method is to rationalize the inequity by cognitively distorting the ability of the comparison other. "I'm just not as good, and therefore I don't deserve the same rewards."

♦ Another way of restoring equity is to quit the organization. Some people cannot bear to be treated unfairly, so they move to a different school.

The key to understanding equity theory is to realize that the perception of the teacher feeling the inequity is all that matters. If a principal does not perceive inequity, but the teacher does, then the principal must deal with the teacher's feelings or risk lowering the teacher's motivation. Dealing with the teacher's perception doesn't mean that the principal has to agree with it. It does mean that the principal needs to speak with the teacher about it and try to explain another perspective. Open, honest, and caring communication is essential if principals are to use Equity Theory effectively to motivate others.

Consider the following two examples. In both examples, see how the principal could use Equity Theory to keep a great teacher motivated.

Example 1

You're working at your desk after school one day when one of your best teachers, Mr. Ramirez, comes in to see you.

After chatting about the day and about how the students responded to instruction, Mr. Ramirez tells you that he is frustrated because two different parents mentioned in passing this week how great the previous year's teacher was. Mr. Ramirez goes on to explain how hard he works to be the best teacher possible and how frustrated he gets when he keeps hearing about last year's teacher.

Example 2

After a faculty meeting, one of your best teachers, Ms. Johnson, asks to speak with you for a moment. She states that she really wanted to chair this year's School Improvement Committee, and she describes her confusion about your choice of one of her colleagues to chair the committee. Ms. Johnson goes on to explain that she feels she has the best qualifications and experience to chair this committee, and she feels slighted that you did not choose her.

In each of these examples, the teacher perceives an inequity. How you deal with this perception needs to be individualized and should be based on your knowledge of the teacher. However, for the purpose of illustration, here are some possible thoughts you may have.

In the first example, Mr. Ramirez clearly is frustrated and somewhat jealous of the attention another teacher receives. Assuming that he is one of your best teachers, you may need to remind him of some of the great things that are regularly said about him. Perhaps you need to help Mr. Ramirez choose a different comparison other. Maybe the teacher Mr. Ramirez is comparing himself with has been at the school longer and has amassed a larger following. Maybe the other teacher is a little bit better than Mr. Ramirez. Maybe Mr. Ramirez has misinterpreted the comments made by a few parents, and he needs to have them explained to him differently.

Regardless of which of these scenarios is true, you must deal with Mr. Ramirez's feelings. You must listen carefully to him and help him restore equity in his own mind. Recognizing that we all want to be treated fairly, you need to help Mr. Ramirez understand the fair treatment that he does get. He must be made to feel that he receives his share of accolades.

The principal who offers a few minutes of time and a compassionate listening ear should be able to help Mr. Ramirez reach this point.

In the second example, Ms. Johnson feels a similar inequity. This situation is slightly different in that you, the principal, are the source of Ms. Johnson's feelings of inequity. Whereas in the previous example your focus was on helping Mr. Ramirez see that he may be misinterpreting things or he may be forgetting some great things said about him, here you need to focus on explaining yourself to Ms. Johnson in a way that will stop her from feeling that she has been treated unfairly. For many principals, these situations are more difficult because of their natural inclination to become defensive. You must resist the temptation to *defend* yourself and focus instead on *explaining* yourself.

In this situation, Ms. Johnson needs to understand why you chose her colleague for committee chair. Perhaps you did so because of the numerous obligations Ms. Johnson already had. Maybe you were trying to help her. Perhaps you wanted to give the other teacher a needed boost of motivation. Perhaps the other teacher really was better suited to chair the committee. Whatever the reason, Ms. Johnson deserves a caring explanation, the focus of which must be on helping her to cognitively restore equity.

In situations like the two just mentioned, you must take great care to avoid discussing other people inappropriately. Although you may be tempted to explain that somebody else was chosen for an honor because of some personal needs, doing so may be indiscreet. The principal must explain the situation in a way that will help restore the perception of equity while also maintaining appropriate confidentiality. It's like Covey's "loyalty to the absent" theory. When we are loyal to the absent, that is, when we don't talk behind people's backs, we retain the trust of those who are present.

A Final Thought about Motivation

We always tell people that the best way to find out what motivates somebody is to ask. Although this may seem overly simplistic, principals are wise to really try to discover what it is that motivates teachers, particularly great ones. Once they have this information, principals should work hard to make these motivators regularly present in the work environment. For some teachers, it's the little things, like positive notes in their mailbox. Others appreciate public recognition for their efforts. Some people find motivation in the occasional box of doughnuts placed in the teacher's lounge. The key point is to discover what motivates teachers and then work hard to deliver it.

One of the best ways to retain quality teachers is to keep them motivated. Theories are important, but nothing replaces good, old-fashioned common sense and the desire to make the work environment fun, rewarding, and motivating. All principals can do that.

Section IV

Adding Quality

9

Adding Quality—
Expanding Our Pool

Teacher turnover is a concern for many schools and districts. It consists of two basic components: losing teachers and replacing the teachers who depart. In previous chapters we discussed a variety of reasons why a teacher may leave. We also pointed out that a teacher's departure may not be inherently negative; in some cases, we welcome it. This chapter focuses on replacing teachers. At the same time that we work to reduce the departure of quality teachers, we need to make sure that we replace any losses with teachers who are at least as effective, if not better. Chapter 10 will follow up on these ideas by addressing how we can position ourselves to keep our newest staff members and diminish the dynamic of teacher departure.

Searching for Irreplaceables

In Chapter 2, we attached labels to teachers of differing quality. The rarest of these are the Irreplaceables; if one of these teachers leave, we will be hard-pressed to find someone as good. But any time a staff member leaves our organization, we want to find the best possible replacement. Doing so can ease the pain of staff turnover. How can we find these elite staff members?

First of all, we must look for them. Many educational leaders tend to settle for available employees instead of working harder to find the best. As we all know, it is much easier in the long run to hire a great teacher than to fire a poor one. Yet in many schools and districts, our hiring skills can be refined. A crucial first step is to ensure that everyone has the same incentive to hire quality.

If I serve as personnel director in a school district that consistently faces a myriad of openings, I may see my primary task as "filling" those positions. I might be tempted to think that my job is done when every slot is full. Although this is true to some degree, it is a disincentive to seeking out excellence. At the building level, effective school leaders understand that the failure to find outstanding employees will add to their burden, not lessen it. At the same time, principals may be tempted to make a decision so they can cross it off their list. If we are to find and employ outstanding teachers, we must make sure that everyone involved in the hiring process has the same goal.

Even at the building level, other factors can prevent us from making the best decision. For example, if I know I am retiring, being moved to another school, or actively seeking another job, I may not be quite as highly motivated to be selective in hiring. I no longer have a vested interest. Let us now consider some other factors that can influence our decisions.

The Emotional Pull

One challenge that faces everyone involved in hiring is the emotional pull. For example, someone's cousin, sister, daughter, neighbor, or spouse applies for a job. We may be tempted to hire the applicant because of the relationship—but this can keep us from making the best decisions. If you think that school board member will like you better because you hire her nephew, wait until you have to put the new employee on an improvement plan!

However, it is equally important to make sure that you do not overlook someone outstanding solely because you feel pressured. A consistent focus on adding the very best quality can help you look at your options in a more neutral fashion.

This emotional pull can also come from within your school. A substitute teacher may regularly bring in cookies for the teacher workroom; a student teacher may have formed close relationships with other staff members. You may feel pretty unpopular if you decide not to hire either of these people. But you have to weigh the pressure of this one-time decision against the pressure of dealing with a lower-quality teacher every day—and their peers would probably be upset with that outcome as well.

An even more challenging situation arises if an applicant is the spouse of one of your teachers. You may be reluctant to offend someone you work with every day by not selecting this applicant. At the same time, you know the consequences of hiring a less effective teacher. Obviously, you will have to balance the talent and quality of the two spouses in making this decision. However, people of the highest quality do realize the challenges that their employers face in such situations and are unlikely to pout or throw a fit if things do not go their way.

Emotional tugs are very difficult for everyone, but especially for educational leaders. We are caring people; we work hard to keep from hurting other people's feelings. All of us hope that others will like and respect us. No one wants to disappoint others. But when we step back and examine what is best for the students in our districts and schools, we remember that this is what will gain us the most credibility—and allow us to sleep best at night!

The Known Quantity

Another factor that may cause us to be less diligent in our quest for excellence is the known quantity—someone on hand who we know will "work out just fine." A classic example is the substitute teacher who works in a school on a regular basis. We may go ahead and hire that familiar person simply because we know what we are getting. This is a great approach if the substitute is an outstanding educator—but it's more likely that the person will just work out.

In situations like these, if we settle for a known quantity of average quality, we pass up the opportunity to add someone great. Even worse, we may have added to our staff someone who will never be particularly effective—and will never leave. Remember that we don't want to focus our efforts on retaining Replacement Level staff members. A strong corollary is that we don't want to hire them if we can do better.

Although people tend to view the challenge of retention as an issue in urban settings, it can also arise in rural communities. The people responsible for hiring in a small community or a less populated area may be tempted to hire "someone who will stay"—that is, someone with local ties. This can work out well if the person hired is an outstanding teacher. But the flip side of "someone who will stay" is "someone who will never leave." In a situation where local ties mean new staff members may well stay for the remainder of their careers, it's essential to seek out candidates of very high quality.

Hiring People Better Than Ourselves

Another challenge facing many people in leadership roles is a resistance to hiring truly outstanding people. Some instinct says, "You don't want to hire anyone better than yourself." What lies behind this resistance? One of the primary reasons may be that the very best people have exceptional judgment. When a principal makes a decision, the best teachers know whether it was a good decision or not. All of us have had the experience, at one time or another, of making a decision we regret. On those occasions, the people we least want to see are probably our best staff members, because we know *they know* we goofed. Thus, leaders who lack confidence in their decision making may not want Irreplaceables in their organization; they may find them too threatening.

This is not all bad news. Let less effective leaders hesitate to hire, or retain, the Irreplaceables. That leaves more great teachers for the rest of us! And if we consistently look for the very best, we can overcome any personal insecurities by reminding ourselves that more effective employees eventually make us look better, too.

The Good Fit

Every educational leader wants to have an environment where people work successfully together. Infighting and confrontation are never much fun. And yet, a core concept of hiring tells us to resist the temptation to choose someone who will just fit in.

When we hire new teachers, we don't want them to fit in and become like our school. Instead, we want our school to become more like them. In other words, no matter how good our school or district is, we want to add people who will raise the average. If this is not our goal and our outcome, then we are hiring the wrong people.

Sure, it's a good idea to hire people who fit in well with other teachers. But it's a much better idea to hire people who are outstanding teachers. If we want to improve our organization, we must seek new talent. The new people may be a little bit of a threat to others, but we will quickly realize that they are not a threat to the others who are good. Of course, we should think of our current organizational dynamics every time we hire a new staff member. But our focus should be on improving the dynamics, not on sustaining the dynamics.

Arbitrary Factors— Narrowing the Pool

An essential element in hiring outstanding teachers is to keep our focus firmly on the central issue of talent and ability. Now, there are many ways to define talent and ability; each of us will determine the definition that best fits our own organization. However, we must take care not to let irrelevant, preconceived notions cause us to overlook qualified candidates.

Must a candidate have a master's degree? Will you look only at applicants with at least two years of experience? Arbitrary requirements such as these reduce your pool of potential new teachers. It may be true that most teachers benefit from some teaching experience, but a truly talented novice soon makes up for the lack of experience. If experience were the chief predictor of success, we would do most of our recruiting at the local senior citizens center.

Finally, we must be aware of our own likes and dislikes. We may prefer candidates with high grade-point averages, or people who participated in extracurricular activities, or applicants who look trim and athletic. We may have had better luck with graduates of certain colleges. Although these inclinations can and will shade our views to some degree, we must take care not to define our pool of candidates on any basis other than the contributions they can make to our setting. The best way to increase our odds of finding effective employees is to maximize our range of options.

Understanding Our Needs

One of the most important determinants of the hiring process is defining the type of educator we need. Traditionally, we have described openings in terms of department or grade level. We commonly think, "Our position is in seventh-grade science, so we need a seventh-grade science teacher." This is true if we are simply looking to fill a position. But if we truly seek to develop an outstanding school, we must focus on consistently hiring great teachers. If we set our sights on hiring superstars, then even if we just get close, our school is likely to grow in the desired direction.

Unfortunately, like most things of value, the process of employing outstanding faculty members takes a great deal of work. If we undertake the task with the expectation of hiring a great teacher, we are more likely to succeed.

It is important to consciously recruit quality candidates. Educators at professional conferences or meetings often rub shoulders with other leading educators. Building relationships with teachers in other schools and areas can open connections to potential future candidates or to people who may know of strong candidates. Making and establishing regular contact with university supervisors of student teachers is another method that can prove fruitful. Contact them as soon as the possibility of an opening occurs; ask if they have any outstanding teacher candidates this year or in the recent past. One way to determine whether these potential teachers can meet your expectations is to ask if any of them are among the best student teachers they have ever had the opportunity to work with.

10

Finding and Choosing the Best

If you have avoided all the potential pitfalls described in Chapter 9, you have a pool of candidates that is as rich and deep as you can possibly get it. Now the obvious question is, "How do I find and pick the best?" There is no precise definition of teacher effectiveness. However, researchers have found certain characteristics that the most effective teachers tend to possess (Stronge, 2002). How can we most effectively find these quality teachers once we have developed our potential candidates?

When hiring staff, educational leaders should always look at the leadership ability of the candidates and the way their personalities will fit into the rest of the school team. Knowing how this person will informally interact with the other faculty members can be an important element in the qualities they can provide a school. Involving other teachers, especially if the new staff will be on a team, can also help insure the effectiveness of the relationships in the working environment.

If organizational leaders consistently pursue the standard of great teachers, they are much more likely to raise the talent level and abilities of the teachers in their schools. Because the standard of greatness is the minimum we can have for the educational settings of our youth, each piece that is a part of the whole must be at that level also. Inducting new staff members and cultivating their ability to become positive school leaders go hand in hand and are important responsibilities of the effective educational leader.

There are some specific things that can increase our chances of success. Although these steps take time, they make it possible for you to select the very best among your applicants.

The Screening

Screening choices involves looking through your applicant pool, highlighting the most desirable of these potential employees, and deciding whom to interview. Factors to consider include transcripts, written recommendations, candidate statements, letters of application, and so forth. Everyone will look at these factors differently. Here, we'd like to move on to address the next step—calling references. This may be the most essential part of the preinterview process, and yet it is easy to cut corners on this step.

The Reference Check

Contacting references takes work, but it can be a make-or-break factor for the hiring of the best candidate. As potential employers, we have the option of contacting no references, one or two, or a dozen or more. This may depend more on our commitment and desire to truly find the best candidate than on an inherent skill. There is a strong relationship between the number of references contacted and the ability to hire effective staff members. Although your district and/or state may have procedural or legal guidelines that you should be aware of before you do reference checks, it's important to contact not only some of the people listed by the candidate but also some others. Your purpose is to determine whether this person is of the caliber you really want for your organization.

If you ask general questions, you will likely get nonspecific answers. "Is he a good teacher?" "Yes, he's a good teacher." What does that mean? I have no idea. Most educators, when called for a reference, will describe everyone as a good teacher.

A more specific inquiry might be, "On a scale of 1 to 10, where would you rank this person?" Ordinarily, you can expect everyone to score at least a 7, if not an 8, 9, or 10. But ask a follow-up question. "How many other 8's do you have in your school?" "How many 9's? How many 10's?" The responses will help provide a much clearer perspective.

Similar questions to ask references might include the following: "If you were named principal at a new school, would you hire this person?" If they answer positively, then ask, "If you were principal at a new school, would you actively recruit this person?" If the answer is affirmative, then ask, "Would this be the first person you would recruit from your current school? Second? How many others would you try to attract before this candidate?"

These questions are not meant to replace specific questions you might have about instructional style, ability to work with others, and the like, but they may help differentiate more specifically the talent level of a potential employee.

Finding the Leaders

The truly elite teacher can make other colleagues better. Hiring a staff member at this level increases the likelihood that the new teacher will improve your school. You don't want just a good social studies teacher; you want a great social studies teacher who can lead others toward that same level. Pursue this line of questioning when contacting references.

Ask references whether this person is a leader. More specifically, ask how many other leaders work in their school, or how many people this teacher was able to influence in a positive manner. Some candidates are uniters; others are dividers. Ask references—whether they were identified by the prospect or not—if anyone on the faculty dislikes this teacher. If so, who? (Not by name, but by quality. Are they the best teachers or the less positive teachers?) How many? Why? Is this teacher likely to get along with colleagues in a new setting?

The Neutral View

All of us have employees we would hate to see leave—and employees we would love to help pack. Although we may truly attempt to be honest and straightforward, our view of any current employee may be tainted. Keep in mind that the person you are calling to inquire about the skills of an applicant may not be entirely neutral. But an employer may be much more able to give a neutral view of a *former* employee. The former employer no longer has a vested interest in retaining (or facilitating the departure of) the person.

Your applications process may require candidates to provide letters of recommendation and names of people who know them. Other people not listed by the candidate—people who may not be current supervisors—can also provide useful information. You may need to get permission from applicants to contact people they have not listed, but many places do this routinely. These secondary references may be able to contradict or affirm the views of others. This extra effort can go a long way toward hiring effective staff members. Wouldn't you rather do the work before you hired someone than wish you had after the person joined your faculty?

Interview Questions

Dozens of Web sites and many other resources list interview questions and strategies. These can give you a working pool of questions. But understanding the purpose of interview questions can also be of value. In contrast with Chapter 9, where the point was to maximize our pool of potential employees, in this chapter we address the task of differentiating among applicants. By contacting references and asking specific questions, we begin to narrow the field. The interview takes us further toward our goal. We need to ask questions that make people seem different, not questions that make people seem the same. Let's look at examples in terms of people you know—your current teaching staff.

Would You Know Whom to Hire?

Take a look at a list of possible interview questions. Now ask yourself this: "If I asked each of my current teachers this question, would their answers tell me who was most effective and least effective?" If the answer is no, this is probably not a good question. If the answer if yes, then you may be onto something.

Let's look at a classic interview question: "What is your philosophy of education?" If you asked 20 teachers this question, would you begin to be able to differentiate their effectiveness based on their answers? No teacher would reply, "I warn the students once and then slam them against the wall!" Yet, most of us know someone who would do that, at least figuratively. The question simply doesn't reveal the teacher's attitude.

Now, you might ask that question just to make the candidate feel more comfortable. That makes sense—but making every candidate feel comfortable doesn't help you narrow the field. So, what should be your approach? You should ask situational questions that are basic and true to teaching. Here is an example.

What Would You Do If?

Give a candidate (or, for that matter, each of your current teachers) the following scenario: "Let's say it is the first week of school, and you don't yet know every student's name. While you are teaching class, one of the students sitting in the center of the room is talking. What would you do?"

Is that a differentiating question? No matter what the teacher responds, then ask, "A few minutes later, the same student is talking again. What would you do?" Follow that question with, "And then a few minutes after that, the same student is talking again. What would you do?" Will these questions differentiate among teachers? They sure will.

How do the best teachers respond? Something to this effect: "Whenever I am teaching, I am up and moving around the room. When the student starts to talk, I would make sure not to give that student more attention. I would take subtle steps that would not be more of a distraction to the other students. I might try to make gentle eye contact. Eventually I would move closer to the student and try proximity. I would continue teaching, but I might have to move close enough that I could put my hand on the student's shoulder."

Ineffective teachers take approaches that tend to escalate more than deescalate the situation. Their initial reply may be the same, but when prompted about the student talking again and then again, they often head in a different direction. Eventually, tactics such as "I would stop teaching class and stare them down" or "I would ask the student, 'Do you want to teach the class?'" will begin to crop up.

Every person's answer will be different, which is of course what you want. But the answers to situational questions help you distinguish between more effective teachers and their less effective peers. Situational questions work because people answering them tend to fall back on what they would really do. When we think about the area of classroom management, we believe that all teachers do the best they know how. Any teacher who *could* improve student behavior in the classroom *would* do just that.

Situational questions can really get to the core of a person's belief system. But it is essential that we do not present outlandish situations. Some educational leaders use "trick" situations or unlikely scenarios. These may make the most effective people look bad. The very best teachers don't give much thought to what they would do if their entire class revolted. It simply would never happen. I know of interviewers who ask questions like, "What would you do if a student lit up a bong in your classroom and started passing it around?" The best teachers have no idea; they simply do not expect this to happen. And, as scary as it may seem, your poorest candidates may be able to rely on experience!

Again, think of how teachers you know well would answer your questions. If you couldn't determine the effectiveness of current staff members based on their responses, the questions most likely won't help you differentiate among prospective teachers.

Setting Expectations

In Chapter 11 we will discuss the induction of new teachers. One key principle is that we must begin the induction process during the interview. Otherwise, we may have missed our chance on certain issues. During the interview, we have the opportunity to set expectations for potential candidates. People want to associate with a winner. High-quality teachers want to go where they feel they can make a difference. An essential component of hiring and retaining superstar staff members is to set expectations for them and their role in the school. This starts during the interview.

Do You Want to Be the Best?

We have always asked potential teachers, "Do you want to be a part of the best school in the country [state/county/city]?" We tell them, "If you do, this is the place to be. We are going to be the best—and you are going to help us get there."

This approach can help establish expectations for the candidate and thus help reestablish expectations for the school. By taking this approach, you not only find out who wants to be at that level, but you also filter out who is at that level and who is not. Asking candidates whether they want to reach excellence can help you identify the applicants you want to pursue and also who really wants to pursue the opening you offer.

Keep in mind, though, that no matter what you do during an interview, you want every potential candidate to leave the interview wanting a job in your school or district. Identifying a tremendous prospect is of little benefit of the candidate doesn't view your organization as a good place to work. Even a less promising applicant may have a roommate, relative, or friend who might consider applying; you never know. Every organization needs as many positive spokespeople as possible. The interview is a valuable time to showcase your organization in the best possible light.

11

Inducting New Teachers

So, now that we have new teachers on board, how are we going to keep them? Teacher attrition is particularly high among teachers in their first few years of service (Ingersoll & Smith, 2003); research has shown that many teachers depart the profession early in their careers (Lortie, 1975; Murnane, Singer, Willett, Kemple, & Olsen, 1991). This issue has gained significance recently as the pool of qualified applicants has shrunk.

The opportunity to fill an open position may be a principal's most precious commodity. The approach the school leader takes when selecting teachers and orienting them to their jobs will greatly determine the school's future direction. Although principals sometimes consider only the hiring process when employing a new faculty member, the education—both formal and informal—they experience after joining the staff is equally important.

New teachers are often chomping at the bit to make a difference. They have never griped in any teachers' lounge; they have no expectation of "following the language of the teacher contract." With staff members who are new to the profession, you may have more of a chance to cultivate them in your image than you do with someone with previous experience. Sometimes leaders hesitate to employ first-year teachers because of potential "growing pains," or because novice teachers may need more support as they establish classroom management. But if you do a good job in the selection process, these people are often very willing to be molded into setting a new dynamic in the school.

In addition, it may be easier to pair inexperienced teachers with your best teachers, setting them on the right track to becoming Solid or even Irreplaceable. Brand new teachers often seek role models; establishing this link early on can help raise the group norm in your school. The other challenge for the educational leader is to maintain these high expectations for the new staff members and to help these new staff members influence others. Keeping their morale at the original high level of excitement is a critical part of the leader's role. Enhancing their abilities to influence previous staff members is also very important.

New Staff Induction and Orientation

Duke (1989) found that acquiring a competent teaching staff is integral to a school's instructional effectiveness. The principal must play a key role in recruitment, inservice education, and staff motivation. Capable, skilled, and energetic teachers must be selected and made aware that their talents will be appreciated. After a robust faculty has been hired, it must be maintained and nurtured with ongoing staff development designed by teachers. The staff must be treated as professionals and encouraged to take leadership positions. If a school does not have proficient teachers, its instructional effectiveness is doomed.

Staff openings are very precious; principals must treat them as such. Making sure that new faculty understand the role they need to play in order for the school to continue to be more effective is very important in the hiring process. Sharing with interviewees that there is no pecking order in the school, that their opinions are as valuable as those of any other staff member, and that they are expected to focus continually on what is best for students can help establish and refine an appropriate environment in a school.

When adding new faculty, the principal should make sure the rookie teacher is influenced in a positive manner. Assign the new staff member a classroom located next to a teacher who will provide productive influence. Arrange the newcomer's schedule around a conference period shared with staff members who can help shape an appropriate belief system. During the interview and hiring process, make it clear to new faculty members which teachers on the staff they should look to for guidance. Explain the need for new staff members to assume needed leadership roles in the school. It is important to establish this expectation early.

When hiring a new staff member, the principal must establish guidelines and expectations. Having a dialogue like this can be an important first step:

- ◆ "I do not believe in pecking orders in our school. I believe that all staff members are of equal importance. When I hire new staff, I want them to take a vocal leadership role in the school. I expect them to speak up at faculty meetings. Within their department (or grade level or team) it is essential that *all* staff, especially our new members, voice their opinions."

- ◆ "If I did not want you to assume a leadership role in the school, I would not have hired you! You have wonderful ideas and are tremendously talented. I need and expect you to take a very visible role at staff meetings and other times when you feel you have something to contribute. I hired you because I want our entire school to benefit from your talents and knowledge."

Having this conversation as part of your first contact with a new staff member can be very empowering. It can give them the confidence to express their opinions and can help their influence infiltrate the school beyond their classrooms.

The principal should make new faculty feel included as early as possible; using available time prior to the start of school is a valuable opportunity (Whitaker, Whitaker, & Lumpa, 2000). As a good first step, invite new staff members to meet with one of your best teachers, or arrange for positive teachers to contact them. Meet with the new teachers, find out what supplies they might need, and support them by providing as many as possible. Taking them out to lunch is one way to help the teachers quickly feel that they are a part of the school and staff. This informal time can also provide additional opportunities to talk about curriculum, philosophies, and management styles of both the principal and the new staff member.

We always enjoyed taking new staff members out to lunch at a nice local restaurant. Imagine the look on their faces when we walked up to our table to find, neatly folded on their plate, a staff T-shirt and business cards with the school logo and their name professionally printed. Talk about a positive start to their school year! Our secretaries were happy to sneak out to the restaurant early to make these arrangements. This morale booster can represent another step to building tremendous loyalty between the principal and the new staff member.

Mentor Programs

Many states and districts offer or require formal mentor programs for new faculty members. This is a wonderful concept, but in practice it is only as good as the mentors themselves. The building-level leader and the central office must make sure that new teachers get the most effective mentors possible and that the mentors receive appropriate training. These critical components of a mentor program dramatically escalate the possibilities of success.

We may be tempted to rotate mentors to be fair to our veteran staff members; we may even be obligated to do so by contract. But we must take steps to establish a good peer relationship for every new staff member. Offering other opportunities at the building level to supplement the formal mentor program may enhance its effectiveness regardless of the official mentor assigned to a new teacher.

Chapter 14 will include further discussion about the importance of induction and the value of a purposeful and continuous mentoring program. The way principals orient new teachers to their school has a direct impact on whether the new teacher's experience is stressful or fulfilling. When principals have the opportunity to add new staff, they must not only hire outstanding candidates but also structure their initial contact with the school to support positive interactions among staff members and foster the relationships that will best influence the new staff and the entire school.

Ongoing Orientation

The best way to support, develop, and cultivate an attitude of lifelong learning in new teachers is through an induction program (Wong, 2002). Organizational leaders should offer a robust new-faculty development program for all rookie staff members. Whether or not they have teaching experience, newcomers should become familiar with the expectations of appropriateness in the school where they now work. Weekly meetings for the first six to nine weeks of school provide one avenue for building collegiality among new staff; they also allow the principal to cultivate effective relationships with the freshman faculty as well as expose them to the staff leaders who offer good role models.

We find it appropriate to hold approximately eight meetings (at 7:15 A.M. every other Tuesday) at the start of the year for new faculty. Sessions focus on a variety of topics ranging from classroom management to the role of the counselor. Spreading the sessions over 16 weeks has proved more manageable than compressing a flood of information into two or three days before the start of school. But the meetings are about more than content. They also aim to build relationships between new staff and the school's most positive and productive staff members and to offer ongoing contact with the principal.

Consider presenting a session on classroom management, led by two of the most effective, positive teachers. Involve your most talented counselor in a discussion of the counseling program. Assign a particularly effective special education teacher to work with new staff. This approach not only orients new faculty to your school's policies and procedures but also encourages them to build relationships with the "right" staff members—relationships that support positive growth among your faculty. When several new staff members come on board in any year, these meetings will help them form a cohesive group and work together toward the new and higher standards you hope they establish.

One of the sessions could offer new staff members the opportunity to evaluate you—a wonderful way for them to interact with you regarding the evaluation process and to see you in the role of a teaching peer.

In another session, before the start of school, you could load the new staff members in one vehicle (a school bus if needed!) and drive them around the community, especially the neighborhoods where your school's students live. This will help give them a feel for the area and provide them with some perspective regarding the home situations of the students they will work with. You might invite other key staff members to be the tour guides or join you on the journey.

Cultivating Leadership

Administrators should talk openly and honestly with new and existing faculty about leadership and the need for it. This should start primarily in one-on-one or small group discussions, but eventually it will involve the entire faculty. It is important that as new staff members join the faculty, they become part of the ever-growing influential direction. Eventually, the entire staff will move over to the positive side of the fence. Like most growth and change activities in schools, this task cannot be accomplished without the leadership of the school's informal teacher leaders. Successful principals have learned to identify the informal leaders and use them effectively to move their schools in a direction that benefits students. Adding new staff members with these skills, and then cultivating these skills, is an essential part of effective staff selection and induction. Shifting the focus from hiring a good teacher to adding a great teacher-leader changes the context in which educational leaders operate.

This principle applies whenever we hire new staff members. A team leader at a middle school can benefit immeasurably when a dynamic teacher joins the team. Adding one or two positive staff members can trigger a sea change across the entire fourth grade or throughout the high school English department. Whether you are a principal hiring a teacher or the head custodian adding a worker to the night shift, the personalities you choose can have a much broader effect than you might realize. It is much easier—and much more enjoy-able—to hire a great employee than to fire a mediocre one!

If we work hard to employ and integrate an outstanding teacher into our school, we'll have a much better year. And if we manage to retain that teacher, we won't have to repeat the effort the next year to fill the same slot. For all these reasons, hiring and inducting new teachers may be the most important part of our work as principals.

Section V

The Impact of Other Stakeholders

12

Supporting Teachers in Parent Interactions

Perhaps one of the most challenging aspects of being a teacher is dealing with difficult parents. Although the best teachers in your school probably spend less time doing this than others, at one time or another every teacher has to deal with a difficult parent. This fact represents one more opportunity for school leaders to enhance the work life of their best teachers. By training teachers in techniques that minimize the likelihood of encounters with difficult parents, and by appropriately mediating between difficult parents and teachers, principals provide a great service that will lead to a better perception of teaching as a career in which to remain.

Cheers or Boos

Before we continue, we must emphasize one point. The best way for a teacher to minimize the frequency of interactions with difficult parents is to be a superstar. Although this will not eliminate all of the difficult parents, it will certainly reduce the number of encounters with them in any given school year. The best teachers, those who consistently show care and concern for children, have far fewer difficult parents to deal with than their less effective colleagues. This makes sense; just look at sports teams for an analogy. The home crowd rarely boos the teams that consistently win. This is true even if the players all earn millions of dollars. However, if a player who is squeezing the payroll with a 20-million-dollar salary consistently fails to perform, people start booing.

Great teachers rarely draw boos from the crowd. But because they care so much, they worry about every boo they hear. This is why principals must make every effort to assist them in dealing with difficult parents. We must protect our superstars from unwarranted booing. We also need to remember that an Irreplaceable teacher, accustomed to cheers, will most likely be troubled by even one boo among a throng of cheers. Principals should anticipate this and be ready to help these teachers remember the hundreds of cheers they have received.

Soothing the Savage Beast

In *Dealing with Difficult Parents: And with Parents in Difficult Situations* (Whitaker & Fiore, 2001), we set forth several techniques for responding to angry, uncooperative, and/or belligerent parents. First, however, we set the stage by delving into the steps that all schools should take to improve parents' perceptions and thus reduce negative interactions. Rather than summarize all of these techniques and skim through a long list of methods out of context, in Section V we aim to provide an overall understanding of the most important elements. Finally, we emphasize the essential requirement that principals do all they can to make teachers feel supported in parent interactions. At the end of this chapter, we explain the subtle differences between *being supported* and *feeling supported.*

Although all teachers would benefit greatly from training in the techniques and ideas described in the following sections, we need to keep our attention focused on our best teachers. These teachers—the ones we care most about retaining—want positive relationships with all parents. Even though the best teachers do everything in their power to foster positive relationships, difficult parents can still get the best of them on occasion. We offer the following suggestions to soothe these savage beasts.

Never let 'em see you sweat. It is important to appear confident and self-assured whenever you are dealing with a belligerent person. In other words, it's important not to give this difficult person any reason to think that she has gotten the best of you or he has made you nervous. Despite your best efforts, though, your voice may become shaky after a confrontation with an angry parent. One of the best ways to combat this is to lower your voice. Teachers with great classroom management skills can confirm that lowering one's voice does more than just hide nervousness. It also helps point out to the angry, loud person just how loud his or her voice is.

Look 'em in the eye. Similarly, when confronted by an angry or belligerent person, we often automatically look down. Because one of our goals is to appear confident, we need to do just the opposite and look the person in the eye. Studies have shown that maintaining strong eye contact often reduces the other person's anger. At the very least, maintaining eye contact demonstrates that you are listening and that you care about what the other person is saying. The best teachers in our school will readily accept this; "caring" is their middle name.

"Sorry" seems to be the hardest word. There is an old saying that the best way to have the last word is to apologize. Our best teachers, though they make the fewest mistakes, apologize regularly. These conscientious teachers routinely apologize for even the slightest errors or misperceptions. Now, we've all been in situations when we know an apology would go very far with difficult parents, but we just don't believe that we've done anything wrong. For these occasions, we train teachers to say, "I am sorry that happened." This doesn't mean admitting any guilt or taking the blame for something the teacher didn't do. In reality, the teacher is sorry that the situation happened, whatever it was. For example, if a teacher punishes a child for talking during a test, and the parent calls to complain, the best teachers really are sorry that the situation happened. Although the punishment was warranted, and even necessary, the teacher is sorry because now a parent and a child are upset. Remember, our best teachers don't like to see people upset. So the teacher expresses sympathy, and the parent hears an apology, yet the integrity of the teacher's actions is maintained—all because the teacher knows how to use the simple phrase, "I am sorry that happened."

Why didn't I know? Although the best teachers in our schools are generally masters at managing their classroom learning environment, now and then the administration may have to take part in handling a student disruption or habitual offense of a classroom rule. In these situations, we must avoid a common pitfall; we must not allow something to escalate to the point of the principal's involvement without ever having let the parent know. Obviously, in some cases an office referral is swift and immediate. We're not referring to those situations here. But if a student's misbehavior or lack of responsibility has gradually escalated to the point where the principal is called in, parents usually ask, "Why didn't I know about this?" This question is more difficult to answer than it is to forestall. To assist teachers in maintaining positive relationships with parents, we need to remind them to stay focused on strong communication skills. They should notify parents early on if a student is having difficulty. This not only helps to avoid the difficult question, "Why didn't I know?" but also helps to establish the teacher as a strong communicator. Parents see this in a positive light, and good communication may even reduce the teacher's number of encounters with difficult parents in the first place.

Staff Development Focused on Parents

One of the best ways to assist teachers in dealing with parents is to educate them about parents and family life in modern times. Just as parents incorrectly perceive some of what happens in schools and then complain about situations that they don't really understand, educators sometimes incorrectly perceive family life and the challenges facing contemporary parents. It's important to remember that, for the most part, educators come from good families with fewer difficulties. Although teachers do not escape their share of tragedies and challenges, the majority of our teachers come from stable home environments free of serious economic difficulties.

Although there is never any excuse for parents to be rude, belligerent, or disrespectful, we do think that it's helpful for educators to know some of the reasons why parents can behave this way. As Stephen Covey reminds us, we should seek first to understand and then to be understood.

Presented briefly and in sketchy detail, here are points school leaders should share with teachers as part of a staff development program focusing on understanding and cooperating with parents. For greater detail, see *Dealing with Difficult*

Parents: And with Parents in Difficult Situations (Whitaker & Fiore, 2001).

- In 1940, fewer than 9% of all women with children worked outside the home.
- Recently, the Bureau of Labor Statistics reported that 78% of women with children between the ages of 6 and 16 were in the labor force.
- Girls with positive paternal involvement are three times less likely to become teenage mothers.
- Boys with positive paternal involvement are less likely to grow up unemployed, incarcerated, or uninvolved with their own children.
- The U.S. Bureau of the Census (1999) reports that 5.6% of U.S. children under the age of 18 are living with their grandparents. Of these, 36% have no parents present in this household. These 1,417,000 children have only their grandparents to rely on for care.
- In 1998, the number of American children under the age of 18 who lived in poverty was 14.5 million (U.S. Bureau of the Census, 1999).
- In families with a female head of household and no husband present, 41% of the children live in poverty.

Although these bits of information focus exclusively on the changes in family dynamics that have taken place in recent years, teachers must understand that we do not offer these facts as a means of judging parents today. The information simply serves to show that life is more stressful for many people than it used to be. This realization does not make it acceptable for parents to be difficult, but it does offer teachers an opportunity to view parents a bit more compassionately.

Furthermore, parents today have much more exposure than ever before to misconceptions about our schools—a fact that may help to explain why so many of them are difficult to deal with. Consider two books that reported very strong sales in recent years: *How Parents Can Save America's Failing Schools*

(Pierce, 2002) and *Bad Teachers: The Essential Guide for Concerned Parents* (Strickland, 1998). In fairness to the authors, these books do not target schools or teachers. Their titles, however, can lead some parents to believe that our schools are in trouble; they could be considered a call to arms for parents who need to save our troubled schools. Principals who share this information with teachers may help them to understand why some parents are difficult and may lessen the stress that these teachers feel when having to deal with them.

Do They Feel Supported?

We have spoken with many school principals who report that one of the most important parts of their job is to support teachers. This is particularly true when working with parents. Teachers say they want support, and principals invariably state that it's important for them to support teachers. We think that a key point is missing here: Supporting teachers is important, but what's really important is making teachers *feel* supported. That's why it's so essential for principals to be aware of people's perceptions. As building principals, we always felt that it was our responsibility to make our best teachers feel supported in their interactions with parents and others. When teachers knew that we were always available, they could come to us with concerns, and we would listen and offer requested advice so that they felt supported. This feeling was comforting to teachers, and we believe it made them more willing to take risks and communicate openly with others. Had the teachers not felt supported, they would have been much less likely to share difficult information with parents, even when this needed to happen. Nobody wants to have a difficult conversation without knowing someone will back them if things become challenging.

The best news in all of this is that your Irreplaceables are pretty easy to support. Because we really need to focus on retaining our best teachers, and because this chapter deals with the major challenge of relationships with parents, isn't it comforting to realize that your best teachers will be easier to support in this regard? Parents respect your best teachers. Your best teachers usually do the right thing with students. Making these teachers feel your support is not a difficult thing to do.

The importance of helping teachers *feel* supported should not overshadow the need to support teachers whenever possible. All those principals who believe that supporting teachers is a critical component of success are correct. However, these principals would be better served to remember that teachers should *feel* supported even when the principal may not fully support the teacher's actions. The feeling of support is a critical component of teacher retention because the best teachers are less likely to continue working in an environment in which they do not *feel* supported.

13

Nurturing Student–Teacher Relationships

Ask any great teacher, "What do you like most about teaching?" The most typical answer will have something to do with the kids. Our best teachers derive great satisfaction from their students, and their relationships with students mean a great deal to them. Similarly, when we ask teachers why they left education altogether or, at the very least, left their particular school, they often cite the challenge posed by student behavior as one reason.

When teachers have difficulty maintaining student discipline, a day in the classroom can seem like an eternity. In a study conducted at Virginia Commonwealth University, researchers Janine Certo and Jill Fox found that many teachers in the metropolitan Richmond, Virginia, area were driven out of the teaching profession because of difficulty controlling student behaviors and the challenges of maintaining student discipline. One teacher interviewed for this 2001 study is quoted as saying,

> I have a reputation for maintaining very strict discipline in my classes.... I've actually seen students drive teachers out with emotional problems and all. I think that maintaining discipline is absolutely crucial, and I'm not sure that it's something you can teach. (p. 43)

Feelings like the one just expressed are not confined to metropolitan areas. In a study summarized in a 2002 article from *Phi Delta Kappan*, negative changes in student behavior and attitudes were ranked as a close third behind the pressures of standards and high-stakes testing and mountains of paperwork as reasons given by teachers with five or more years of experience for leaving the teaching profession. One teacher in this study stated,

I had looked forward to teaching and hoped that it would be my pleasure to assist in the learning process of elementary students, but many students just don't seem to care about learning and really cause disruption for those who do. Since there was no separating these students, the serious ones had to pay the price. Watching their gradual decline in enthusiasm was very difficult…we were all powerless. (p. 30)

Clearly, nurturing the student–teacher relationship is key to attaining the expected joys and rewards of teaching. Having the skill to do this is one of the things that separate good principals from great principals. The great ones provide guidance to teachers, particularly early in their careers, that assists them in nurturing relationships and in managing the learning environment. Great principals also serve as role models by nurturing positive relationships with students themselves.

Recognizing Success in Student–Teacher Relationships

One of the ways in which we improve any skill we've been working on is to have somebody recognize any level of success we may have already attained with the skill. For example, think of a child learning a new skill. A toddler's first step brings thunderous applause from parents, siblings, friends, and anybody else who may witness the event. They continue to express this joy and pride with each new step until walking has become automatic. The same is true when a child first learns to speak. Any approximation to real words elicits excitement and praise from the child's eager parents. "Dada" is one of the most joyous sounds a new father ever hears, and the sound is typically reinforced until it evolves into "Daddy," which quickly becomes the most joyous sound. But what if the new father reacted with little or no enthusiasm to the sound "Dada"? What if the child received a response indicating that "Dada" was the correct label, but no accompanying encouragement or prompting to lead to "Daddy"? Chances are the child would not learn to speak as quickly and would not derive as much pleasure from using correct words as if the parents offered praise and support.

It may seem silly to spend time writing about language acquisition and walking in a book about retaining quality teachers, but the concept of nurturing relationships and recognizing efforts at improving them is essential to making teaching rewarding and is really analogous to child development for a couple of reasons. First, all quality teachers possess the initial desire to form positive, productive relationships with students, just as all children possess the initial desire to walk and talk. Second, all quality teachers have had some training in forming these positive, productive relationships with students, just as all children have had some training in walking and talking. In both of these cases, most of the training comes in the form of modeling. Preservice teachers spend weeks in the classrooms of experienced teachers observing student—teacher interactions and relationships. From birth, children watch their parents and other family members walk and talk, and they quickly realize that these are two necessary skills for survival.

Finally, and most important, the degree to which quality teachers receive recognition and feedback as they strive to form positive relationships with students is directly related to their success in nurturing these relationships with all students, just as the recognition and feedback a young child receives for early attempts to walk and talk is directly related to the child's desire and ability to continue to develop these skills. Whether we are speaking about children or adults, recognition for efforts at improvement and growth are essential to motivation. In Chapter 5, we described Frederick Herzberg's Hygiene-Motivation Theory. This theory, you'll recall, states that recognition and achievement are two great motivators for people. A September 2002 article in *Principal Leadership* drives this point home clearly. In writing about specific things that principals can do to retain teachers, the author states, "Teachers who choose to remain in teaching report that their greatest reward is student success" (p. 53). Principals, therefore, should search for ways to point out students' successes, particularly in terms of the relationships teachers have been skilled at forming with them. Teachers greatly appreciate these observations and "pats on the back." As a teacher named Sharon states in the same *Principal Leadership* article,

> He [the principal] has been extremely supportive. He is acting as a mentor role model, guiding me through, tapping me on the shoulder when needed. He uses subtle ways to make you think about what you are doing. At the same time he gives you pats on the back when needed. He's good. (p. 53)

Student–Teacher Relationships and the Six Types of Teachers

In Chapter 2, we wrote about six different types of teachers to help school leaders determine the quality and effectiveness of their existing teaching staffs. Often, once we begin to objectively assess the quality of the teachers currently employed in our schools, we can get a much clearer understanding of which faculty members need assistance with student–teacher relationships. Just as important, we can discover which faculty members would not accept or benefit from any assistance. These faculty members—often the Replacement Level faculty members—cannot be the focus of our efforts at nurturing student–teacher relationships because focusing on them would be futile at best. This is particularly true with the faculty members we would classify as Negative Forces. Although the Negative Forces on any faculty must be prevented from doing harm to students and from forming overly negative relationships, the nature of these teachers is to be negative. We don't need to concern ourselves with retaining these teachers. Instead, we need to show them the door.

One of us worked with a teacher earlier in our career whom we'll call Warren. Warren was the most Negative Force on this particular faculty, and he took great delight in interacting negatively with students, parents, colleagues, and administrators. Warren's negativity was exacerbated by the fact that he had several colleagues who would be classified as Harmless (recalling the classifications presented in Chapter 2). Although Warren's Harmless colleagues rarely initiated negativity in their interactions with students themselves, they served as a willing audience to Warren's tirades in the teachers' lounge and to his stories about how each particular class was more rotten than the ones that came before. This audience was exactly what Warren needed to fuel his own negativity. As we know, the most negative people, whether teachers, parents, or students, feed off other people's reactions to their negativity.

Dealing with people like Warren can be time-consuming and draining. But it need not be as time-consuming and draining as some of us make it. There is no question that we must manage the Warrens of the world. We must not permit their negative attitudes to cause students, or others, harm. But we cannot let the Warrens become the focus of our efforts. On every faculty with a Warren or two, there are also Irreplaceables and Solids. These are the people whose relationships with students must be nurtured. It is with these teachers that a principal can make the most difference.

Nurturing Solid Relationships

The best teachers on your faculty—the Irreplaceable ones, the ones you must be most concerned about retaining—don't tend to need any assistance in nurturing relationships with students. In fact, these teachers typically enjoy positive relationships with everybody—students, parents, and colleagues. This is one of the aspects of their personality that render them Irreplaceable. But because teachers do cite relationships with students and the challenges of effectively managing behaviors and learning environments as reasons for leaving the teaching profession, all school leaders need to concern themselves with assisting the Irreplaceable teachers when students and situations present unusual challenges. In other words, we do not need to focus our efforts to nurture student–teacher relationships on the Irreplaceable teachers, but we should support them, and they should feel that support, on the rare occasions when they do find student behavior difficult to manage.

Solids, on the other hand, should be the focus of our efforts in this area. We should help Solids develop the skills to improve and enhance their relationships with students. The Solids—the largest percentage of almost any faculty—have the potential to become truly great. They tend to work very hard, and they are at the greatest risk of leaving the profession if their hard work doesn't lead to gains or improvements. If the principal recognizes a Solid for efforts to form positive relationships with students and to manage the learning environment, then the Solid will feel a sense of satisfaction and motivation, as explained by Herzberg. But recognition, though important, is not enough. Principals should also focus all their professional development efforts on the Solids. These professional development efforts ought to include readings, workshops, or meetings that target issues of student behavior and classroom management.

As with all aspects of teacher retention, the principal is the key player when it comes to helping teachers in forming rewarding relationships. To retain the highest quality teachers, principals must recognize the innate human need for relationships. By nurturing relationships, principals have the power to make teaching a fulfilling career choice. Because most quality teachers mention students as a primary source of their career satisfaction, it is only natural for school leaders to want to do everything in their power to give teachers the tools necessary for rewarding relationships with students. This means more than just ensuring that teachers receive training and are then recognized for their success in forming positive relationships with students. It also requires that principals form positive relationships with students, demonstrate skill in managing student behavior, and deal with classroom disruptions effectively. As noted in Chapter 7, principals are role models. Keeping the best teachers on board requires that principals model effective techniques and genuine concern for relationships. Doing so can have a dramatic effect on teachers' feelings of satisfaction with their profession.

14

Building a Family Atmosphere through Purposeful Mentoring

In Chapter 11, we introduced the concept of inducting new teachers and briefly explained the importance of mentoring. During this introduction, we presented the case for ensuring that a rookie teacher is influenced in a positive manner. In even the best schools, there are negative staff members who often find it challenging to resist the temptation to gripe, complain, and speak negatively about parents, students, administrators, and colleagues. The principal must ensure, as we pointed out, that new teachers are sheltered from these negative influences to the greatest extent possible. It is the principal's responsibility to provide a mentoring relationship between new teachers and the most positive, skilled teachers already on the staff. This responsibility cannot simply be an assumed one, however. Instead, principals need to understand some basic facts about inducting new teachers, and they must have some training and expertise in structuring a mentoring program that will be successful and not too difficult to implement.

Induction That Sticks

From beginning to end, this book is about keeping our best and brightest teachers teaching within our schools. Unlike other books that focus on the topic of teacher retention, we choose to differentiate between retaining quality teachers and simply retaining all teachers. With that in mind, recall that a hallmark of our best teachers is that they want to be the best teacher they possibly can be. Our best teachers were likely to have been exceptional preservice or student teachers, and as they entered the teaching profession, their strong desire was to quickly become the very best teachers. The challenge facing these folks is that the transition from preservice superstar to the real experiences that go with the first year of teaching "is perhaps the most complex intellectual and emotional transition on the continuum of teacher development" (Steffey et al., 2001, p. 4).

In response to these truths, more school systems have begun studying their induction practices for new teachers (Fideler & Haselkorn, 1999). As a result, teacher induction has received a great deal of attention, and staff development offices in school systems all across the country have begun focusing greater efforts on providing induction to new teachers. Although school systems should be applauded for these efforts, having an induction program is not the same as having a quality induction program. Induction cannot be viewed as something we do at the beginning of a new teacher's tenure with us simply because doing so is the trend. Instead, efforts must be focused on providing induction that will really mean something to new teachers and that will stick with them as their careers continue.

Making induction stick really isn't any different from making any form of staff development stick. The best principals in this country recognize that before designing a program for staff development, they need to find out what development the staff needs and wants. Then, they need to ensure that training is delivered by highly qualified trainers in a manner that is least intrusive on the staff members' other duties. Finally, the best principals recognize the need for regular follow-up—opportunities for teachers to continue dialoguing about the development, as well as a built-in system of evaluation that will provide meaningful feedback about whether the staff development efforts have met their objectives.

Such programs stand in sharp contrast to one-shot staff development offerings. Weaker principals schedule staff development opportunities that seem meaningful, only to turn around and plan something completely unrelated the next time around. Because many principals are not given the autonomy to design their own staff development programs for their schools, the same critique of staff development planning and implementation can be levied against those charged with staff development at the school system level.

In the best schools, principals create induction programs that address what new teachers really want and need to know. They do this not because of their supreme knowledge about what new teachers need and want, but because they include other teachers in the planning and design of induction. The best principals ask their best teachers what they wish they had known when they began teaching. Furthermore, they include their best teachers in the delivery of any teacher induction activities. Finally, they ask for immediate feedback from new teachers after the induction program to discover what they still didn't know or weren't prepared for.

To create an induction program that really sticks, principals need to first believe that an induction program can make the difference between new teachers staying in the profession or leaving for another more fulfilling career. Of course, induction cannot do this alone; it must be paired with meaningful mentoring. But the strength of induction that sticks is that it responds directly to what new teachers need; therefore, it does increase the likelihood that new teachers will find the induction experience helpful and worthwhile. As Podsen (2002) stated in *Teacher Retention: What Is Your Weakest Link,*

> The bottom line is this: A strong support system for a beginning teacher, an experienced teacher new to your school, or an experienced teacher making the transition into another career stage, can make the difference between the teacher staying or leaving, and will have your school fostering the type of career development that results in highly productive and self-actualized professionals. (p. 60) (National Teacher Recruitment Clearinghouse, 2000)

We are certain that all the readers of this book want to keep the best teachers teaching in their schools. Who among us wouldn't share that goal? As you face the golden opportunities of adding quality to your faculty when you hire new teachers, pay attention to the kind of induction you give them. As the saying goes, you never get a second chance to make a first impression. Induction is a first impression for your new teachers. To keep the great ones, do everything in your power to make that first impression stick.

Why Focus on Mentoring?

Virtually every industry in America has increased its focus on mentoring programs in recent years. The need to offer guidance, support, and assistance on the job, by a colleague, has become a universally recognized need in the workplace. Even outside the workplace, there has been increased discussion about the value of mentoring. Not only do workers benefit from mentors but so do members of society at large. In fact, just last week we saw two different celebrities on television talking about the importance of adults mentoring children in their communities. The workplace has seized the concept; Hollywood has jumped on the bandwagon; and schools, in particular, have recently stepped up their efforts to mentor new teachers in some very profound ways. The impact of these school-based efforts is that teacher attrition, particularly for our best teachers, has begun to drop substantially. Effective mentoring can make it easier to keep your best and brightest on board.

But what is mentoring? Of the many definitions of mentoring and mentor programs, we find India Podsen's (2000) one of the best:

> Mentoring can be defined as a sustained relationship between a novice and an expert. In a clearly defined teacher-mentoring relationship, the expert provides help, support, and guidance that helps the novice develop the necessary skills to enter or continue on his or her career path. As a mentor, you have two main roles, as an expert and as a role model, in your teaching field. (p. 4)

Even school leaders who understand what mentoring is sometimes question whether the time and effort that goes into creating a meaningful mentoring program actually produce the desired results. As Darling-Hammond (1999) discovered through her research, states that have introduced high-quality mentoring programs have found that attrition rates for new teachers dropped by more than two-thirds from their previous levels. It is safe to assume that some of the teachers previously lost to attrition might have developed into Irreplaceables had they received some guidance early on. Because an Irreplaceable teacher wants to become the best teacher possible as quickly as possible, programs that offer collegial assistance are extremely important. Even when a mentor program does not assist in teacher development, mentors can be of great service simply by explaining policies and procedures and introducing the new teacher to other members of the staff.

As pointed out in Chapter 11, you must take great care when choosing teachers to serve as mentors within your school. Just as successful induction programs need to involve the best teachers, choosing the best teachers to act as mentors sets the stage for the teachers being mentored to adopt some top-notch behaviors and skills. But the choice of teachers as mentors is only part of the puzzle. The other, perhaps even more important, part of this whole teacher development puzzle is to train the mentors in the skills they need.

Mentoring the Mentors

Mentor teachers must understand what the role requires of them, and they must be willing to accept the myriad responsibilities that go along with mentoring. It is likely that the best teachers on your staff will welcome these responsibilities, because they tend to have a strong desire to impact the learning of all children within their schools. It is less likely, however, that your best teachers will automatically understand the true role of a mentor.

The role of a mentor teacher goes by several different names, depending on the formality of the school's mentoring program. Whether we're talking about a buddy teacher, a support teacher, a cooperating teacher, or a mentor, one thing is clear. Mentor teachers, to be most effective and contribute positively to a new teacher's development, must receive some type of formal training. The many skills required of a successful mentor can be too complex to master without guidance. In fact, Wagner (1985) points out that we cannot simply assume that a teacher who performs well with children will be adept at teaching adults. Therefore, we need to start mentoring our mentors.

Recall that our focus is on keeping the very best teachers. This requires that we choose the very best mentors possible for these teachers. To maximize the mentor's chances of exerting a positive influence on teaching habits and skills, we should partner teachers with mentors who teach the same, or at least similar, grade levels or subject matter. This increases the likelihood that the interaction between mentor and new teacher will focus on substantial issues, not just on learning each other's curriculum or content.

Because mentor teachers are required to assist new teachers with both procedural duties and more technical, teaching-related duties, it's important for principals to provide some training in both of these areas. If we have chosen our very best teachers to be mentors, then the teaching-related duties will likely not need the most attention. If truth be told, our best teachers could teach us a thing or two about effective teaching. Nevertheless, principals should offer mentor teachers some training of a pedagogical nature, because even if they are outstanding teachers themselves, there are likely differences in the teaching styles of the new teacher and the mentor, and these differences ought not to be limiting in any way. Even our best teachers can benefit from having different methodologies or procedures for lesson delivery explained to them from time to time.

However, the procedural duties of teaching may actually be more difficult for our best teacher mentors to explain to new teachers. Our best teachers may take many of the daily procedures (attendance, dismissal duty, grade recording) for granted if they choose, instead, to devote their energy and their thinking to more substantive, instructional duties. Principals must work with mentor teachers to ensure that they carefully explain and reinforce these procedural duties with the teacher being mentored.

Finally, it's a good idea for principals to advise mentor teachers about what research most often describes as the important qualities for mentor teachers. The list below, the direct result of a study of mentor and new teachers (Tickle, 1994), is divided into three categories: professional qualities, personal qualities, and tutorial qualities.

Professional Qualities

- *Credibility as a teacher*
- *Experience*
- *Continuous learner*
- *Open to learning from colleagues*

Personal Qualities

- *Empathetic*
- *Sensitive*
- *Nonjudgmental*
- *Approachable*
- *Sense of humor*
- *Good listener*
- *Calm manner*
- *Optimistic*

Tutorial Qualities

- *Accessible*
- *Positive constructive nature*
- *Supportive/encouraging*
- *Honest*
- *Reliable*

(Tickle, 1994)

In the final analysis, the principal has responsibility for building strong mentors. When mentoring programs fail, they fail because principals don't realize their own responsibility for making them work. Principals need to choose the right teachers as mentors and then train and support them so that they can best serve the new teachers. Principals who do this are far more likely to create mentoring programs that will make a difference to new teachers—and maybe even lead the best ones to a state of fulfillment as teachers.

When Does Mentoring End?

We'll admit it right now; this is a trick question. In the best schools, under the leadership of the best principals, mentoring never ends. Think about it: Until we reach the point that every member of our staff performs at the highest possible level, we need to keep mentoring active. This awareness makes the difference between the best principals and the least effective principals as they work to retain quality teachers. Although the data indicate that the number of mentoring programs our schools offer is on the rise, far too many mentoring programs still have a defined beginning and a defined end. To compound the problem, many of these mentoring programs end sometime during a new teacher's first year! We don't know about you, but neither one of us ceased to need mentoring, support, guidance, or assistance after only one year as a professional educator. We doubt that even our best rookie teachers reached that point so early.

To combat teacher attrition and keep our best and brightest teachers on board, principals must stop viewing mentoring as a program and start seeing it as part of their schools' culture. Teaching is a demanding profession; its nuances challenge even the most experienced master of the trade. If we can create school cultures that value continuous growth and learning, our teachers will have a better chance of meeting these challenges. If principals can recognize the need to continuously pair staff members in learning teams that allow for the growth of both parties, maybe teachers will be less vulnerable to stagnation and burnout. Further, if principals can engage in a mentoring relationship themselves, perhaps with an administrative colleague, someone at central office, or a professor at a nearby college, then they can begin modeling the kind of lifelong learning, growing, and mentoring that teachers need to see.

The induction and the subsequent mentoring of new teachers are keys to their success in the short term and their fulfillment in the long term. Principals who choose mentors from the ranks of their best teachers are far more likely to see ongoing improvement throughout their teaching staff—a great by-product of mentoring. Mentoring not only increases the stability of a school's teaching force, but it also significantly increases the likelihood of retaining the best and brightest teachers in the school.

15

Teaching:
The Most Important
Profession

Retaining quality teachers is an awesome, yet necessary, responsibility for school leaders to assume. As we said in the opening of this book, the stakes are higher now than ever before. The need for quality teachers to meet the new standards and to ensure that all children learn, and learn well, is more apparent today than in any previous era. There is only room for great teachers today; no school, no matter how high its test scores, can afford to lose the great ones.

As we've said from the beginning, the real issue is not teacher retention. The real issue is retaining quality teachers—keeping the best and brightest on board. By recognizing who the best teachers are, and by focusing on the environmental factors that often lead these teachers to choose a departure from teaching, school leaders will be positioned to keep the best teachers in their schools. We hope we have given you some things to consider about making your school the type of school that teachers want to work in. Principals have tremendous power to create the right environments and to combat some of the biggest reasons teachers give for leaving the profession.

In a nutshell, it all comes down to recognizing that teaching is the noblest profession. It's important that all school leaders recognize this fact—but even more important that they make teachers aware of that recognition. Teachers need regular reminders that the work they do is valuable and more significant than most other professions. The best teachers in your school, the Irreplaceable ones, will feel honored if the leader consistently and genuinely pays tribute to the work they do. To assist you in this regard, we offer the following list of quotes. Our selection is not an exhaustive list, but it does illustrate what people from various walks of life and in various eras have said about education and teaching. Sharing these with your teachers can lead to some great discussions about the nobility of their work. We hope that you find something of value in this list, and we thank you for doing your great work to ensure that all of our teachers are excellent ones.

> An understanding heart is everything in a teacher, and cannot be esteemed highly enough. One looks back with appreciation to the brilliant teachers, but with gratitude to those who touched our human feeling. The curriculum is so much necessary raw material, but warmth is the vital element for the growing plant and for the soul of the child.
>
> *Carl Jung*

You can pay people to teach, but you can't pay them to care.

> *Marva Collins*

The mediocre teacher tells. The good teacher explains. The superior teacher demonstrates. The great teacher inspires.

> *William Arthur Ward*

A master can tell you what he expects of you. A teacher, though, awakens your own expectation.

> *Author unknown*

Example isn't another way to teach; it is the only way to teach.

> *Albert Einstein*

Teaching is not a lost art, but the regard for it is a lost tradition.

> *Jacques Barzun*

The true teacher defends his pupils against his own personal influence. He inspires self-distrust. He guides their eyes from himself to the spirit that quickens him. He will have no disciple.

> *Amos Bronson Alcott*

He who dares to teach must never cease to learn.

> *Richard Henry Dann*

The teacher who is indeed wise does not bid you to enter the house of his wisdom but rather leads you to the threshold of your mind.

Kahlil Gibran

Effective teaching may be the hardest job there is.

William Glasser

Teachers who inspire realize there will always be rocks in the road ahead of us. They will be stumbling blocks or stepping-stones; it all depends on how we use them.

Author unknown

Teaching kids to count is fine, but teaching them what counts is best.

Bob Talbert

I touch the future. I teach.

Christa McAuliffe

From teachers and trainers we need willingness to try a style that perhaps isn't theirs by birth, but which works for their learners. The challenge for teachers and trainers is to combine the old content with the new approaches.

Marc Prensky

A teacher affects eternity; he can never tell where his influence stops.

Henry Brooks Adams

The man who can make hard things easy is the educator.

Ralph Waldo Emerson

The teacher is one who makes two ideas grow where only one grew before.

Elbert Hubbard

To be good is noble, but to teach others how to be good is nobler—and less trouble.

Mark Twain

I am indebted to my father for living, but to my teacher for living well.

Alexander the Great

The dream begins with a teacher who believes in you, who tugs and pushes and leads you to the next plateau, sometimes poking you with a sharp stick called truth.

William Arthur Ward

I am not a teacher, but an awakener.

John Sculley

The good teacher...discovers the natural gifts of his pupils and liberates them by the stimulating influence of the inspiration that he can impart.

Stephen Neill

The best teacher is the one who suggests rather than dogmatizes, and inspires his listener with the wish to teach himself.

Stephen Neill

It is the supreme art of the teacher to awaken joy in creative expression and knowledge.

Edward Bulwer-Lytton

You cannot teach a person anything; you can only help him find it within himself.

Galileo

Education is not the filling of a pail, but the lighting of a fire.

William Butler Yeats

The pupil who is never required to do what he cannot do, never does what he can do.

John Stuart Mill

I'm not a teacher: only a fellow-traveler of whom you asked the way. I pointed ahead—ahead of myself as well as you.

George Bernard Shaw

A gifted teacher is as rare as a gifted doctor, and makes far less money.

Author unknown

The art of teaching is the art of assisting discovery.

Mark van Doren

Teacher's Prayer

I want to teach my students how
To live this life on Earth,
To face its struggles and its strife
And to improve their worth.
Not just the lesson in a book
Or how the rivers flow,
But how to choose the proper path
Wherever they may go.
To understand eternal truth
And know the right from wrong,
And gather all the beauty of
A flower and a song.
For if I help the world to grow
In wisdom and in grace,
Then I shall feel that I have won
And I have filled my place...
And so I ask your guidance, God,
That I may do my part
For character and confidence
And happiness of heart.

James J. Metcalf

Retaining Quality Teachers

History will show that the focus in education shifted somewhat early in the 21stcentury. It remains to be seen whether the remainder of this decade, or even of this century, will keep us as focused on accountability and the concept of success for all. Also still unclear are the questions whether "No Child Left Behind" will sustain itself as an educational mantra and whether all schools can achieve universal proficiency. Finally, we cannot say with certainty that all teachers can be transformed into outstanding teachers.

It must be noted, though, that during this decade we shifted our focus away from the idea that we needed to retain teachers, away from the explosion of research and studies predicting a teacher shortage. Let it be said that the focus on teacher retention was missing a key component—until this book came along. This book, we hope, shifts the focus away from the issue of teacher retention and toward the objective of retaining *quality*teachers. This book was born of a desire to assist all school leaders in recognizing quality, cultivating quality, and maintaining quality.

History will also show that real school improvement in the 21stcentury came about when we finally began paying attention to the great teachers and doing all we could to retain them. If we want great schools, then great principals will need to stay focused on great teachers. Focusing our energies on mediocre teaching will lead to mediocre student learning. Whatever we say about the educational climate today, one thing is clear. It does not focus on mediocrity—and neither should we.

References

Adams, J. S. (1965). Inequity in social exchange. In L. Berkowitz (Ed.), *Advances in experimental psychology*, vol. 2. New York: Academic Press.

Benham Tye, B. & O'Brien, L. (2002). Why are experienced teachers leaving the profession. *Phi delta Kappan, 84*(1), 24–32.

Betancourt-Smith, M., Inman, D., & Marlow, L. (1994). *Professional attrition: An examination of minority and nonminority teachers at risk.* Paper presented at the annual meeting of the Mid-South Educational Research Association. East Lansing, MI: National Center for Research on Teacher Learning. (ERIC Document Reproduction Service No. ED 388639)

Billingsley, B. S. (1993). Teacher retention and attrition in special and general education: A critical review of the literature. *Journal of Special Education, 27*(2), 137–174.

Bissell, B. (1992). *The paradoxical leader.* Paper presented at the Missouri Leadership Academy, Columbia, MO.

Buell, N. (1992). Building a shared vision—The principal's leadership challenge. *NASSP Bulletin, 76*(542), 88–92.

Burr, A. (1993). *Being an effective principal.* Paper presented at the Regional Satellite Meeting of the Missouri Leadership Academy, Columbia, MO.

Certo, J., & Fox, J. (2001). *Retaining quality teachers.* Metropolitan Educational Research Consortium, Virginia Commonwealth University.

Cheng, Y. C. (1993). Profiles of organizational culture and effective schools. *School Effectiveness and School Improvement, 2*, 85–110.

Cherniss, C. (1980). *Professional burnout in human service organizations.* New York: Praeger.

Chittom, S. A., & Sistrunk, W. E. (1990). *The relationship between secondary teachers' job satisfaction and their perceptions of school climate.* Paper presented at the annual meeting of the

Mid-South Educational Research Association, New Orleans. East Lansing, MI: National Center for Research on Teacher Learning. (ERIC Document Reproduction Service No. ED326567)

Covey, S. R. (1990). *The seven habits of highly effective people: Restoring the character ethic.* New York: Simon & Schuster.

Darling-Hammond, L. (1999). *Solving the dilemmas of teacher supply, demand, and standards: How we can ensure a competent, caring, and qualified teacher for every child.* New York: National Commission on Teaching and America's Future.

Delgado, M. (1999). Lifesaving 101: How a veteran teacher can help a beginner. *Educational Leadership, 56*(8), 27–29.

Duke, D. L. (1989). What can principals do? Leadership functions and instructional effectiveness. *NASSP Bulletin, 66*(456), 1–12.

Etzion, D., Kafry, D., & Pines, A. (1982). Tedium among managers: A cross-cultural, American–Israeli comparison. *Journal of Psychology & Judaism, 7,* 30–41.

Fideler, E., & Haselkorn, D. (1999). *Learning the roles: Urban teacher induction practices in the United States.* Belmont, MA: Recruiting New Teachers.

Fiore, D. J. (1999). *The relationship between principal effectiveness and school culture in elementary schools.* Doctoral dissertation, Indiana State University, 1999.

Fiore, D. J. (2001). *Creating connections for better schools: How leaders enhance school culture.* Larchmont, NY: Eye On Education.

Frase, L. E., & Melton, R. G. (1992). Manager or participatory leader? What does it take? *NASSP Bulletin, 76*(540), 17–24.

Friedman, I. (1991). High and low burnout schools: School culture aspects of teacher burnout. *Journal of Educational Research, 84*(6), 325–333.

Friedman, I., & Lotan, I. (1985) *Teacher stress and burnout in Israel.* Jerusalem: Mekhon Henriyetah Sold.

Futrell, M. H. (1999). Recruiting minority teachers. *Educational Leadership, 56*(8), 30–33.

Greenfield, W. D. (1985). *Instructional leadership: Muddles, puzzles, and promises.* The Doyne M. Smith Lecture, University of Georgia.

Greenleaf, R. (1977). *Servant leadership: A journey into the nature of legitimate power and greatness.* New York: Paulist Press.

Herzberg, F. (1975). One more time: How do you motivate employees? *Business Classics: Fifteen key concepts for managerial success.* Cambridge, MA: President and Fellows of Harvard College.

Holmes Group. (1986). *Tomorrow's teachers: A report of the Holmes Group.* East Lansing, MI: Author.

Ingersoll, R. (1998). The problem of out-of-field teaching. *Phi Delta Kappan, 79*(10), 773–776.

Ingersoll, R. M., & Smith, T. M. (2003). The wrong solution to the teacher shortage. *Educational Leadership, 60*(8) 30–33.

James, B. (1996). *The baseball abstract.* New York: Simon and Schuster.

Johnson, S. (1998). *Who moved my cheese?* New York: Putnam.

Kahn, R. L. (1974). *Conflict, ambiguity, and overload: Three elements of stress.* Springfield, IL: C. C. Thomas.

Kim, I., & Loadman, W. (1994). *Predicting teacher job satisfaction.* East Lansing, MI: National Center for Research on Teacher Learning. (ERIC Document Reproduction Service Number ED 383707)

Latham, A. S., Gitmer, D., & Ziomek, R. (1999). What the tests tell us about new teachers. *Educational Leadership, 56*(8), 23–26.

Lortie, D. C. (1975). *Schoolteacher: A sociological study.* Chicago: University of Chicago Press.

Lumpa, D. (1997). *Correlates with teacher and student satisfaction in elementary and middle schools.* Unpublished doctoral dissertation, University of Missouri, Columbia.

Lundin, S., Paul, H., & Christensen, J. (2000). *Fish! Catch the energy, release the potential.* New York: Hyperion Press.

Maslach, C. (1982). *Burnout: The cost of caring.* New York: Prentice Hall.

Maslow, A. H. (1970). *Motivation and personality* (2nd ed.). Reading, MA: Addison-Wesley.

Merrow, J. (1999, October 6). The teacher shortage: Wrong diagnosis, phony cures. *Education Week, 64,* 48.

Murnane, R., Singer, J., Willett, J., Kemple, J., & Olsen, R. (Eds.) (1991). *Who will teach? Policies that matter.* Cambridge, MA: Harvard University Press.

National Association of School Boards of Education (1998). *The numbers game: Ensuring quantity and quality in the teaching workforce.* Alexandria, VA: Author.

National Center for Education Statistics (1997). *The condition of education 1997.* Washington, DC: United States Department of Education.

National Center for Education Statistics (1998). *The condition of education 1998.* Washington, DC: United States Department of Education.

National Teacher Recruitment Clearinghouse (2002). In I. Podsen (Ed.), *Teacher retention: What is your weakest link?* Larchmont, NY: Eye on Education.

Pierce, G. E. (2002). *How parents can save America's failing schools.* Philadelphia: Xlibris.

Pines, A., Aronson, E., & Kafry, D. (1981). *Burnout: From tedium to personal growth.* New York: The Free Press.

Podsen, I. J. (2000). *Coaching & mentoring: First-year & student teachers.* Larchmont, NY: Eye on Education.

Podsen, I. J. (2002). *Teacher retention: What is your weakest link?* Larchmont, NY: Eye on Education.

Recruiting New Teachers. (1998). *The essential profession: A national survey of public attitudes toward teaching, educational opportunity, and school reform.* Belmont, MA: Author.

Sergiovanni, T. J. (1996). *Leadership for the schoolhouse.* San Francisco: Jossey Bass.

Seyfarth, J. (2002). *Human resources management for effective schools* (3rd ed.). Boston: Allyn and Bacon.

Shann, M. (1998). Professional commitment and satisfaction among teachers in urban middle schools. *The Journal of Educational Research, 92*(2), 67.

Shirom, A. (1991). Burnout in work organizations. In Friedman, High and low burnout schools: School culture aspects of teacher burnout. *Journal of Educational Research, 84*(6), 325–333.

Sistrunk, W. E. (1982). In S. A. Chittom & W. E. Sistrunk (Eds.), *The relationship between secondary teachers' job satisfaction and their perceptions of school climate.* Paper presented at the annual meeting of the Mid-South Educational Research Association, New Orleans. East Lansing, MI: National Center for Research on Teacher Learning. (ERIC Document Reproduction Service No. ED326567).

Steffey, B. E., Wolfe, M. P., Pasch, S. H., and Enz, B. J. (Eds.). (2000). *Life cycle of the career teacher.* Thousand Oaks, CA: Corwin Press.

Stolp, S. (1994). Leadership for school culture. *ERIC Digest, 91.*

Strickland, G. (1998). *Bad teachers: The essential guide for concerned parents.* New York: Pocket Books.

Stronge, J. H. (2002). *Qualities of effective teachers.* Alexandria, VA: ASCD.

Tickle, L. (1994). *The induction of new teachers.* London: Cassell.

U.S. Bureau of the Census (1999). Online source: www.census.gov.

Wagner, L. A. (1985). Ambiguities and possibilities in California's mentor teacher program. *Educational Leadership, 43,* 23–29.

Weiss, E. M. (1999). Perceived workplace conditions and first-year teachers' morale, career choice commitment, and planned retention: A secondary analysis. *Teaching and Teacher Education, 15*(8), 861–879.

Whitaker, M. E. (1997). *Principal leadership behaviors in school operations and change implementations in elementary schools in relation to climate.* Doctoral dissertation, Indiana State University, 1997.

Whitaker, T., & Fiore, D. J. (2001). *Dealing with difficult parents: And with parents in difficult situations.* Larchmont, NY: Eye On Education.

Whitaker, T., Whitaker, B., & Lumpa, D. (2000). *Motivating & inspiring educators: The ultimate guide for building staff morale.* Larchmont, NY: Eye on Education.

Wong, H. (2002). Induction: The best form of professional development. *Educational Leadership, 59*(6), 52–54.

If you enjoyed this book, we recommend…

Creating Connections for Better Schools:
How Leaders Enhance School Culture
Douglas J. Fiore

This book demonstrates that student achievement depends on school culture, the one element of your school at the foundation of everything that happens there. School culture is the system of beliefs, values, and expectations that governs the feelings and actions of everybody there.

Practical and accessible, this book shows you what you can do to build relationships and connections to enhance your school's culture. It provides advice about how you can—

- boost your staff's morale
- increase student achievement
- receive the support you need from parents and the community

Included are guidelines to help you:

- communicate with teachers, students, and parents on a regular basis
- be "visible"
- recognize, utilize, and empower your faculty

2001, 165 pp. paperback 1-930556-05-5
$25.95 plus shipping and handling

Order form on page 167

Dealing with Difficult Parents
(And with Parents in Difficult Situations)
Todd Whitaker & Douglas J. Fiore

This book is an easy read with common sense appeal. The authors are not afraid to share their own vulnerability and often demonstrate a sense of humor.

Gale Hulme, Program Director
Georgia's Leadership Institute
for School Improvement

This book helps teachers, principals, and other educators develop skills in working with the most difficult parents in the most challenging situations. It shows you how to:

- avoid the "trigger" words that serve only to make bad situations worse.
- use the right words and phrases to help you develop more positive relationships with parents.
- deal with parents who accuse you of not being fair.
- build positive relationships with even the most challenging parents.

2001, 175 pp. paperback 1-930556-09-8
$29.95 plus shipping and handling

Order form on page 167

What Great Teachers Do Differently: Fourteen Things That Matter Most
Todd Whitaker

This book is a quick read and is packed with good stuff. It is filled with humor that makes the book readable, interesting and "real."

Barbara McPherson, Principal
Stony Point North Elementary School
Kansas City, KS

What Great Teachers Do Differently describes the beliefs, behaviors, attitudes, and interactions that form the fabric of life in our best classrooms and schools. It focuses on the specific things that great teachers do...that others do not. It answers these essential questions:

- Is it high expectations for students that matter?
- How do great teachers respond when students misbehave?
- Do great teachers filter differently than their peers?
- How do the best teachers approach standardized testing?

2004, 144 pp. paperback 1-930556-69-1
$29.95 plus shipping and handling

Order form on page 167

Motivating and Inspiring Teachers:
The Educational Leader's Guide
for Building Staff Morale
Todd Whitaker, Beth Whitaker, and Dale Lumpa

The most appealing feature of this book is its simplicity and common sense. It is practical, useful and readable, and I recommend it.

Ron Seckler, Principal
Swope Middle School, NV

Filled with strategies to motivate and stimulate your staff, this book features simple suggestions that you can integrate into your current daily routines. It will show you how to:

- insert key phrases and specific actions into your day-to-day conversations, staff meetings, and written memos to stimulate peak effectiveness
- hire new staff and plan orientation and induction meetings to cultivate and retain loyal and motivated staff members
- use the "gift of time" to stimulate and reward
- get amazing results by not taking credit for them
- motivate yourself each and every day

2000, 252 pp. paperback 1-883001-99-4
$34.95 plus shipping and handling

Order form on page 167

Great Quotes for Great Educators
Todd Whitaker and Dale Lumpa

Over 600 insightful, witty nuggets to motivate and inspire you…

…and everyone else at your school.

Teachers—display these quotes in your classrooms! **Administrators**—insert them into your faculty memos and share them at staff meetings!

Why is this book unique?

- includes over 100 original quotes from internationally acclaimed speaker and educator Todd Whitaker
- features real quotes from real students, which echo wit and wisdon for educators
- each quote has a direct connection to your life as an educator

Examples of quotes in this book…

Great teachers have high expectations for their students, but higher expectations for themselves.

Todd Whitaker

We can never control a classroom until we control ourselves.

Todd Whitaker

2004, 208 pp. paperback 1-903556-82-9
$29.95 plus shipping and handling

Order form on page 167

Dealing with Difficult Teachers
Second Edition
Todd Whitaker

... filled with inspirational ideas and strategies that work.

Melanie Brock, Principal
Westview Elementary School
Excelsior Springs, MO

Whether you are a teacher, administrator, or fill some other role in your school, difficult teachers can make your life miserable. This book shows you how to handle staff members who:

- gossip in the teacher's lounge.
- consistently say "it won't work" when any new idea is suggested.
- undermine your efforts toward school improvement.
- negatively influence other staff members.

Added to this edition are 4 new chapters on communicating with difficult teachers.
This new section demonstrates how to:

- eliminate negative behaviors.
- implement effective questioning strategies.
- apply the "The Best Teacher/Worst Teacher" test.

2002, 208 pp. paperback 1-930556-45-4
$29.95 plus shipping and handling

Order form on page 167

What Great Principals Do Differently:
15 Things That Matter Most
Todd Whitaker

... affirming and uplifting, with insights into human nature and 'real people' examples...

Edward Harris, Principal
Chetek High School, WI

What are the specific qualities and practices of great principals that elevate them above the rest? Blending school-centered studies and experience working with hundreds of administrators, Todd Whitaker reveals why these practices are effective and demonstrates how to implement each of them in your school.

Brief Contents

- It's People, Not Programs
- Who is the Variable?
- Hire Great Teachers
- Standardized Testing
- Focus on Behavior, Then Focus on Beliefs
- Base Every Decision on Your Best Teachers
- Make it Cool to Care
- Set Expectations At the Start of the Year
- Clarifying Your Core

2002, 130 pp. paperback 1-930556-47-0
$29.95 plus shipping and handling

Order form on page 167

Interested in ordering multiple copies of Eye On Education titles?

♦ Order copies as "welcome" gifts for all of your *new* teachers.

♦ Order copies as holiday gifts for *all* of your teachers.

♦ Assign them as required reading in new teacher induction programs.

♦ Assign them in book study groups with experienced teachers.

Our discount schedule:

			Discount
10–24	copies	=	5%
25–74	copies	=	10%
75–99	copies	=	15%
100+	copies	=	20%

(plus shipping and handling.
Feel free to call for more information)

*Note: These discounts apply to orders of individual titles and do not apply to combinations of more than one title.

Larchmont, NY 10538
Phone (914) 833–0551
Fax (914) 833–0761
www.eyeoneducation.com

ORDER FORM

❏ **Creating Connections for Better Schools: How Leaders Enhance School Culture.** Fiore. 2001. 165 pp. paperback 1-930556-05-5. $25.95 plus shipping and handling.

❏ **Dealing with Difficult Parents (And with Parents in Difficult Situations).** Whitaker and Fiore. 2001. 175 pp. paperback 1-930556-09-8. $29.95 plus shipping and handling.

❏ **What Great Teachers Do *Differently*: 14 Things That Matter Most.** Whitaker. 2003. 130 pp. paperback 1-930556-69-1. $29.95 plus shipping and handling

❏ **Motivating and Inspiring Teachers: The Educator's Guide for Building Staff Morale.** Whitaker, Whitaker, and Lumpa. 2000. 252 pp. paperback 1-883001-99-4. $34.95 plus shipping and handling.

❏ **Great Quotes for Great Educators.** Whitaker and Lumpa. 2004. 208 pp. paperback. 1-930556-82-9. $29.95 plus shipping and handling.

❏ **Dealing with Difficult Teachers, Second Edition.** Whitaker. 2002. 208 pp. paperback 1-930556-45-4. $29.95 plus shipping and handling.

❏ **What Great Principals Do *Differently*: 15 Things That Matter Most.** Whitaker. 2002. 130 pp. paperback 1-930556-47-0. $29.95 plus shipping and handling.

Fill in your address on other side

Please place your check and/or purchase order with this form in an envelope and mail to *Eye On Education*. If you are not satisfied with any book, simply return it within 30 days in saleable condition for full credit or refund.

Ship to: _____
       Name

_____
School

_____
Address

_____
City   State   Zip

_____
Phone   Your title

Bill to: _____
       Name

_____
School

_____
Address

_____
City   State   Zip

_____
Phone   Your title

Subtotal (books)   _____

Shipping and Handling   _____

Total   _____

Shipping and Handling:

1 Book—Add $6.00   2 Books—Add $10.00   3 Books—Add $13.00
4 Books—Add $15.00   5–7 Books—Add $17.00 8–11 Books—Add $19.00

Method of Payment (choose one):

☐ Check (enclosed)   ☐ Credit Card   ☐ Purchase Order

_____   _____
Credit card # (Visa, Master Card, Discover) or PO #   Expiration Date

6 Depot Way West, Larchmont, N.Y. 10538
(914) 833–0551 Phone (914) 833–0761 Fax
www.eyeoneducation.com